The Guerrillas Have Taken Our Son

Chad & Pat Stendal

Dear Paul,

May God bless you.

RANSOM
PRESS
INTERNATIONAL
P.O. Box 1456
Burnsville, Minnesota 55337

Printed in the United States of America
by Ransom Press International
Burnsville, Minnesota

Library of Congress Cataloging-in-Publication Data

Stendal, Chad, 1927–
    The guerrillas have taken our son / by Chad and Pat Stendal.
      p. cm.
    1. Colombia—Politics and government—1974–
2. Guerrillas—Colombia—History—20th century.
3. Kidnapping—Colombia—History—20th century.
4. Violence—Colombia—History—20th century.
5. Stendal, Chad, 1927–   . 6. Stendal, Pat, 1930–
I. Stendal, Pat, 1930– . II. Title.
F2279.S74 1989
986.1'0632—dc19   88–38096
ISBN 0-931221-02-1   CIP

Dedicated to all our Friends and Neighbors
who have been killed, and to those
who continue to suffer under
violent terrorist attacks
in Colombia.

We wish to dedicate this book
especially to our Colombian
co-worker, *Salomon Vergara*,
who was shot and killed by
masked terrorists on the
trail to Mamarongo,
December 6, 1988.

Contents

At least 40 bullets were fired at close range at me in this airplane.

CHAPTER 1

Baptism of Fire

October 31, 1982

It was a peaceful Sunday afternoon in eastern Colombia. I circled my small aircraft and looked around at my three passengers as I prepared to land. This was Antonio's first flight to the eastern plains area of Colombia. A recently graduated architect, he was going to advise me on how best to add a touch of beauty to our functional ranch buildings. Seated in the co-pilot's seat, his head turned constantly as though on a swivel, as the fascinating panorama of scenic beauty unfolded around him.

Below us, areas of grassland alternated with lush rain forest growth along the waterways. The largest of these, the mighty, mud-laden Guaviare River, wound its wide, brown, twisting path through the tropical vegetation, while the smaller streams writhed like small green snakes, overshadowed completely by the trees clustered along their banks.

In the back seat of the plane was a Guayabero Indian woman and her teenaged daughter. The mother had recently recovered from a severe illness. Four months earlier, my son Chaddy had found her dying in her home deep in the jungle. He carried her in a hammock about four miles up the side of a steep rise to a plateau, where I landed my plane and took her to our home for medical attention. Now they were returning to their family.

We had taken off that morning from our home base in the

town of San Martin, about 140 miles to the west. San Martin is a well-established cattle town, founded in 1535 by Spanish conquerors, searching for gold. Our home there, Casa Agape, has been a refuge for sick jungle Indians and homesteaders who needed physical and spiritual help and had little resources of their own.

I landed the blue and white Cessna 182 on a small airstrip cut out of the jungle at the edge of the river. Here my other son, Russell, the oldest of our four children, operated a commercial cold-storage unit, supplying frozen fish to different parts of Colombia. My passengers and I sauntered over to the tin-roofed fish house, while Gustavo, one of Russell's employees, began refueling the airplane. His wife, Rosa, served us small cups of strong, sweet, very black coffee called *tinto*, the customary expression of hospitality in Colombia.

I spent a few minutes talking with a group of fishermen who were visiting Gustavo, then climbed aboard the small plane along with my passengers and taxied toward the turn-around at the end of the little grass runway.

My mind was on the flight ahead of me. Would the weather hold? October and November are noted for their abrupt changes in weather as the rainy season ends and the dry season begins. My destination was 200 miles east to the Indian woman's home.

Fish house on the Guaviare River.

It would be a dangerous flight over jungle most of the way. The sky looked clear, but for some unexplainable reason I felt uneasy. As I turned around, I caught some motion out of the corner of my eye, and suddenly I felt an urge to get out of there. Instead of doing the usual pre-flight checks, I swung the plane around and gave it full throttle.

As the little Cessna gathered speed, two rough-looking individuals stepped out of the jungle onto the narrow strip . At first I thought they were just curious country people who wanted to see the airplane take off. I was horrified when they put submachine guns to their shoulders and started firing at us. The plane was rapidly picking up speed, and the assailants were now only thirty feet away and were shooting point blank into the aircraft. I could see the face of one of the men, grimacing with rage, as he put his shoulder forward into the recoil of the submachine gun. They crouched as the wing tip passed over their heads and gave us a burst right into the door. As we continued our take-off roll, we could hear the gunfire continuing, even after we broke ground and were in the air. Immediately I banked the plane to make a more difficult target, and the firing stopped as we rapidly ascended out of range.

As I completed the turn, putting some trees between me and the gunmen, I glanced into the back seat. From the number of shots that had been fired, I expected to see the sides of the plane looking like a sieve, and the passengers dead or dying. Unbelievably, no one was hit! In fact, there weren't even any holes in the cabin. My architect friend was so pale he looked green, but he was not even scratched. I began to check myself over carefully, as I had heard stories of people being shot and not realizing it during the excitement of a shoot-out. It seemed I was all right, and all instruments were normal.

Then Antonio noticed gasoline gushing out of the right wing tank. The gas was flowing over the right flap, and I noticed that I had not raised the flaps as every pilot automatically does after take-off. Then I remembered that the Cessna 182 had electric flaps, and the flap motor was under the flow of the escaping gasoline. I shuddered as I realized what would have happened had I touched the control lever to activate the flaps. We would probably have sparked the gasoline and blown up in one of those big orange balls of flame that you see so often on television adventure shows.

I left the flaps down and switched to the left gas tank. Fortunately, both tanks had been full, leaving no room for vapor, which is necessary for an explosion.

The woman passenger told me she had seen several more men in the edge of the jungle. I circled the strip from about 1500 feet, but I could see no strangers near the strip. I headed for another airstrip just three miles away, where the jungle turns to grassland. We landed in a hurry and quickly siphoned the remaining gas from the right tank into a fifty-five gallon drum. I knew we had about twenty minutes before the assailants could arrive from the river airstrip on foot.

Then, without warning a line of low, dark, rolling clouds passed right over us, and a cloudburst hit us with such heavy, driving rain that I couldn't see the runway markers, let alone the end of the runway. Fearful that the guerrillas would locate us and begin firing again, I gave the plane full throttle, even though my visibility was almost zero due to the heavy rain. 'Better the rain then the guerrillas,' I thought, and found I could see only enough to make out the change in color of the vegetation where the airplane had worn down the grass by repeated take-offs and landings. When we got to the place where the grass strip had not been used and was all the same color, I knew it was time to pull the plane off the ground.

I pulled it up, and visibility went to zero. I couldn't see the ground, even straight down. I made an instrument turn and after a few anxious moments, we reached the edge of the storm. I pulled up to 3,000 feet, and soon we landed at San Martin.

Fidel, our aircraft mechanic, and I examined the airplane very carefully and found only three bullet holes. One bullet had made the gaping hole in the right wing, totally destroying the gasoline tank rubber liner. The other two bullets imbedded themselves in the door hinge. We dug out two 9 mm submachine gun slugs. The hinge, with the door jamb behind it, was probably the strongest place in the airframe. Had the bullets been two inches higher, they would have easily penetrated the plexiglass and, from their angle of impact, would have entered my chest. Many more bullets were fired. Why had they not hit the plane?

"It was a real miracle," insisted Antonio. "How could the bullets have missed us? I was staring right down the barrels of the machine guns. I could see the flashes coming out of the barrels and hear the discharges as they pointed right at us." He was absolutely convinced that God intervened.

The trauma of this incident was such that several times a day for several weeks, I relived the terrifying incident, seeing again in my mind the grimace on the face of the gunman as he fired point blank at us with his submachine gun flashing.

Two days later Gustavo and Rosa arrived in San Martin. Being too unnerved to remain in the jungle, they closed up the fish house and traveled by canoe and truck to our home. Gustavo told us that after the guerrillas had fired at the plane, they ran straight to our walk-in freezer and house and shouted, "Hands up, everyone! Nobody make a move!"

"Who was in that plane?" the guerrilla leader asked.

"The father of Russell who owns this place," answered Gustavo, adding that I had just brought a load of supplies. The gunmen swore, voicing their extreme frustration at not having been able to stop the airplane.

When they heard the sound of our airplane landing just a few miles away, they demanded to be taken immediately to the other airstrip to try to intercept the plane again. They rounded up all the visitors, together with Gustavo and Rosa, and marched everyone at gunpoint down the airstrip in the direction where our plane had landed. No one was left behind to spread an alarm.

The women were crying; most everyone thought that they were being marched off into the jungle to be shot. They had trudged about half a mile when the tremendous storm engulfed them. When the guerrillas heard the plane take off again, they released their prisoners, and they themselves disappeared into the jungle.

"Those men were not from this area of the jungle," Gustavo told us. "They were strangers to all of the people who were visiting us that day."

We knew that subversives were operating in Colombia, but there had been no incidents in our immediate area. We had thought that if the guerrillas came to our area, they would respect the fact that we had helped so many people with medicines, mercy flights, and aid of every kind. We had no known enemies, only friends in the entire region. Our fish business gave honest work to many people.

After much discussion we decided that the strangers must be part of a guerrilla band who were making a reconnaissance of the river area. We also realized that they had fired at the plane with a woman and child aboard without even knowing who we were, showing themselves to be ruthless with no respect for innocent life.

At that time it was hard to realize that we were dealing with not just a few bandits, but with one of the toughest and most ruthless forces the world has ever seen. Nor did we guess that our whole family was about to be swept into danger.

Chaddy (right) and friend at Chaparral.

CHAPTER 2

Chaddy vs Mrs. Kirby

I had no idea what a crucial turning point lay ahead of us. My wife Patty and I had arrived in Colombia in 1964 from Minnesota. As Christian missionaries we had immersed ourselves in the lives of the Kogi Indians in the mountains of northern Colombia, living in the Indian village of Mamarongo. Ten years later we had extended our ministry to several jungle tribes in eastern Colombia about 500 miles to the south. Our four children—Russell, Chaddy, Sharon, and Gloria—had grown up in Colombia and were involved in various aspects of the work. Until now, we had felt relatively secure in the jungle.

In the days following the attack on our plane, my mind wandered back three years to March, 1980. The ranch, Chaparral, is located on the huge Guaviare River in eastern Colombia and comprises 3,300 acres of grassland. It is the center for our work with the jungle Indians and other operations.

About fifteen miles upstream lies one of the larger ranches of about 20,000 acres called Mapiripan. The owners, Tom and Rickey Kirby, were the only other North Americans to own land in that area of Colombia. They were among the very first to enter the region and were now in their sixties. Somehow Patty and I weren't able to achieve more than a superficial acquaintance with these veteran ranchers from Florida. Tom, who was suffering from crippling arthritis, had little interest in missionary work, and the few times we had encountered Rickey, she had been furiously angry with our son, Chaddy.

The incident that upset Rickey the most happened when Chaddy wanted to cross her land to get to a friend's farm to do

15

some plowing with a tractor. Rickey had locked up the entrance to the road with a big padlock.

Now in Colombia, a common thoroughfare is never supposed to be locked up. However, in this case, Mrs. Kirby had declared the area to be her property, ignoring Colombian custom, and travelers were told to go up to the ranch house (one hour away) and get the key. Then, of course, they had to return to the gate, unlock it, then return the key and come back again to the gate to drive the tractor through. Even assuming that the Kirbys were home and willing to release the key, this totaled several hours. The same procedure was necessary when travelers came back out. So rather than waste alot of time, Chaddy pulled out his six-shooter and blasted the lock to smithereens.

Mrs. Kirby didn't have much trouble figuring out who shot up her lock. The tracks of the tractor were plain to see, and Chaddy had the only tractor in the area. The town of Mapiripan (named for the Kirby ranch) was close at hand, so she went to town and filed a complaint with the police. The town was temporarily without a police inspector, but the policeman in charge went downriver to Chaparral to arrest Chaddy. He planned to take him to jail and hold him until such time as the new inspector arrived, and his case could be tried.

Since Chaddy knew the policeman's temperament, when he came to get him, Chaddy gave him two choices: One, Chaddy would kill a chicken and invite the policeman to dinner. After eating, the policeman would go back to town alone, trusting that Chaddy would arrive without fail the next Sunday to answer to the charge before the new police inspector. Or two, the two of them would shoot it out on the spot. (The *llanos*[1] frontier is the Colombian equivalent of the American wild west a hundred years ago.) Chaddy had helped construct the jail as a community service. It consisted of two tiny cells, neither one built to accommodate his body dimensions, and he figured it would just about kill him to be confined in there. The policeman decided on the chicken dinner and left, as Chaddy figured he would, and Chaddy went to town the next Saturday and presented himself before the inspector Sunday morning.

---

[1]*llanos*— the plains area of Colombia, consisting of rolling grassland with jungle along the rivers. These *llanos* regions border the thick tropical rain forest and are ideal for cattle.

The Kirbys arrived in their new, red Toyota, and the trial proceeded. The inspector asked Mrs. Kirby to state her complaint. Then Chaddy expressed his viewpoint, and tension mounted as Mrs. Kirby took the opportunity to admonish him in English, not only about the gate, but also about the company he was keeping and other matters. She thought to save him embarrassment by communicating in English, but a crowd soon gathered to witness the spectacle of the stocky, gray-haired woman shouting in English at the barefoot cowboy with curly, reddish blond hair, who was translating her comments into Spanish for the benefit of the townsfolk. The inspector, for some reason, thought the case much more serious than it really was. He asked how many fence posts had been stolen and how many meters of fence had been torn down. He was amazed to find out that only the lock had been damaged, and the gate had not even been left open. He settled the case by ordering Chaddy to pay the Kirbys for the lock.

As the Kirbys reached the door after receiving the payment, Rickey turned around and told the inspector that she would really like to see Chaddy ordered to do some community service to pay for his insufferable attitude. She threatened Chaddy with dire consequences if she ever saw him anywhere on her land, except on the main road.

As Chaddy started to leave, the inspector called, "Hey, wait a minute!" He typed out an order for Chaddy to pay a fine and clean the brush and refuse out of a large lot behind the inspection office.

At first Chaddy refused to sign, and the inspector was just ordering him to be jailed, when the young cowboy changed his mind. He signed both copies, put them in his pocket, and promising to be back in a minute, he went out on the street and asked a number of his friends, responsible business and cattlemen, to sign a petition against the order.

Accompanied by his friends, including the president of the Council for Community Action, Chaddy returned to the inspector's office. The council president was the spokesman. "How did you get out here yesterday?" he asked the police inspector after greeting him and welcoming him to the town.

"I was flown out here by a very nice, North American pilot who refused any pay," responded the inspector.

"I can see that you don't know who you are dealing with," continued the president. "That pilot is this boy's brother. They have been respected members of this community for many years. Check your records, and you will find that they were among the first contributors to the construction of this police station and jail. This young man is highly esteemed by this community."

The new police inspector had assumed that the Kirbys were the important people to please in the community. Now at the council president's words, he began to revise his opinion of the situation. "In that case I think I'd better tear up these papers," he replied. (Mrs. Kirby had been the council president in charge of building the new jail.)

After the papers had been destroyed, and Chaddy and the police inspector had shaken hands, Chaddy and his friends went behind the station and completely cleaned out the lot, even plowing it and discing it with the tractor; however Rickey Kirby felt frustrated and indignant over the situation.

The very next day, as Mrs. Kirby was out riding her range, Chaddy happened to see her from the road as she topped out on a hill. He immediately swung his tractor off the road and drove over to meet her.

He jumped off his tractor, whipped off his cowboy hat, and said, "Good morning, Mrs. Kirby, I've come to ask you for a job."

She looked him in the eye for at least a full minute with her hands on her hips where she carried her big pistol. At last she broke the silence, "You've got a lot of nerve asking me for a job after what happened yesterday."

He pointed out that by hiring him to plow some of her land and plant a better quality grass, she would be doing a service for both of them—her pasture and cattle would be improved, and he and his tractor would have employment.

"If you hadn't made Tom so mad yesterday, I'd think about it," she replied as she rode away with the trace of a smile on her face.

One morning a few months later, Chaddy was able to improve his relationship with Rickey Kirby even more. Russell had landed at Mapiripan, and Rickey brought a passenger to the airstrip in her Toyota. She found Russell and Patty waiting for Chaddy who had gone into town. She took this golden opportunity to express herself eloquently to Patty about what she thought of Chaddy. Soon Chaddy returned, and after a few unpleasant exchanges between them, mostly over his refusal to speak English or wear shoes, she got into her jeep. The boys and Patty got into the plane and were just gathering speed down the runway when Chaddy, who was looking out the side window, shouted, "Stop!"

Russell aborted his take-off, and Chaddy bounded out of the plane and over to the Kirby jeep that had almost disappeared into a large hole about eight by six feet and about five-and-a-half feet deep. It had been dug not far from the airstrip during the making of earthen bricks, and was concealed by tall grass. The back tires and last three feet of the jeep were all that were visible above the hole, and the vehicle was almost straight up and down.

Rickey had managed to get out of the driver's window which was well down into the hole, and when the boys and Patty arrived, she was indignantly surveying the situation and expressing herself as to what she thought of the person who made this "elephant trap."

"Don't worry, Mrs. Kirby, I'll get it out for you," Chaddy offered.

"Chaddy Stendal! Don't you touch my jeep!" she retorted and walked off toward town, a short distance away, to get some "real" help.

As soon as she was gone, Chaddy removed the crossbar of a soccer goal post, which was at the edge of the airstrip. With this long, hefty pole inserted under the front bumper, he was able to move the jeep. A large missionary who was waiting for a flight helped the whole operation by adding his weight to the end of the pole. Chaddy then lowered himself into the driver's seat, where he found the keys still in the ignition.

While Russell and some bystanders raised the vehicle to a horizontal position, Chaddy backed it out of the hole. Chaddy then set about to straighten out the dents and indentations in the metal sides and fenders as best he could. Soon the Toyota looked good as new. He took off for town and pulled alongside Mrs. Kirby just as she was arriving at the town's edge.

"Can I give you a lift?" he offered.

Mrs. Kirby got in the jeep and soon after that gave Chaddy the job he wanted. He stayed in the Kirby home for several weeks.

The Kirbys, we eventually learned, were not very happy with the way eastern Colombia was developing. Many complicated (and sometimes even conflicting) laws were on the books, making it almost impossible for anyone with a business to comply with all of them. There were scores of underpaid government workers in overstaffed regulatory offices. These, together with five different agencies of undercover police, were busy looking for violators of the law, not always to enforce justice, but sometimes to obtain bribes that would enhance their income enough to support their families.

Government money appropriated for schools, roads, and hospitals in many frontier areas was often absorbed by corrupt politicians, instead of being put to efficient use. The morale of dedicated and efficient government workers was lowered by the corruption in their midst.

Rickey Kirby had even been asked to pay a bribe to a judge in order that a case concerning her ranch be resolved favorably. What really angered her, however, was the fact that for several years now, *mafia*[2] personnel had been encouraging the local people to plant drugs (cocaine and marijuana). The entire atmosphere of Mapiripan was changing as easy drug money corrupted the citizens. The usual drunken brawls and shoot-outs were now more frequent and more violent.

But unknown to us, onto this exuberant frontier scene, was settling the menacing hand of Marxist guerrillas, bringing with them kidnappings, killings, extortion, and violence. Planning the infiltration of this area from their headquarters far away in the isolated Macarena mountains, they began to send in agents and agitators. The lure of exploiting the lucrative drug industry to finance their Marxist revolution was too great to pass up. Posing as colonists or business men, often running pool halls or saloons where they could observe and hear all the local news, these agents identified those who might later oppose them and therefore had to be eliminated or somehow removed from the area.

Rickey Kirby's name was on the list.

Now our lives and the lives of the Kirbys were about to cross in a bizarre incident that none of us could have predicted.

Out in the jungle, a plan was being set in motion.

---

[2]The word *mafia* refers to drug traffickers.

Russell flew us to Mamarongo in the Cessna 182.

CHAPTER 3

Shepherd or Hireling

January 1983

Three months had passed since my airplane encounter with the guerrillas, but the memory of that October day had not faded. The guerrillas were extending their control into new areas all over the country. The situation had become worse when the government declared an amnesty for all guerrillas, supposedly to return them to civilian life. Hundreds of Marxist guerrillas that had been in jail were set free. Most of them returned to their guerrilla bands, and suddenly the country was beset with a tremendous increase in kidnappings, extortions, and assassinations.

With dismay we learned that bands of guerrillas were now operating in the Sierra Nevada de Santa Marta, a mountain area just off the north coast of Colombia where the Kogi Indians live. Our family had spent many years in these mountains, living among these small, distinctive people, studying their difficult language, and learning their fascinating customs. Now the Indians sent us word that a major epidemic was raging among them. A virulent, bloody dysentery was killing the Kogis, sometimes within twenty-four hours of onset, and they needed help right away. This put us in a very difficult situation. To enter the Kogi area to help the Indians, we had to expose ourselves to possible guerrilla activity.

We went up to the Santa Marta area to consult with the military authorities to see how serious the situation really was.

It couldn't have been worse! A group of guerrillas was operating on each side of the area we wanted to enter. Either band could reach us within five hours once they knew we were there.

We returned sadly to San Martin in the eastern plains country and made the situation a matter of serious prayer. The Lord strongly impressed upon me the Bible story of the wolf attacking the sheepfold. The hireling flees when the danger comes, but the true shepherd stays and protects the sheep. That settled the matter for me. We were not hirelings; we would not flee the danger but would stay and help the Kogis.

We were able to obtain many cases of ampicillin for both adults and children from a pharmaceutical factory. They even gave us a 40 percent discount because the medicine was destined for Indians. I was making an educated guess that the epidemic would respond to a wide-range antibiotic. Actually, if the disease were caused by a virus instead of a bacteria, our medicine would be useless.

Three of us planned to go to the Sierra—Patty; our daughter, Sharon, who is a registered nurse; and myself. Shortly before our departure date we had all fallen ill with a tropical disease called dengue fever. The symptoms of this miserable disease, also known as "break-bone" fever, are sweating, fever, weakness, loss of appetite, and extreme pain in all parts of the body. Over half of the cases include an unbearable itching of the palms of the hands and soles of the feet. It is long-lasting, usually taking a month for recovery, and relapses are common. The mortality rate is about 5 percent, and no specific drug is available.

Patty and I were almost well when the time came to leave for the Kogi area, but Sharon was dangerously ill. Her only relief was to sit with her hands and feet in bowls of ice water, and at that, the pain and itching was just barely bearable. After three or four sleepless nights, we were all at our wits' end what to do. Not only was Sharon's illness delaying our leaving to help the Kogis, but her life now was definitely in danger.

The seriousness of her situation, together with the urgency to get to the Kogis brought me to a strong determination of faith. Difficult and dangerous circumstances must not be allowed to keep us from doing God's revealed will. Of course, we had prayed for Sharon many times before, but now with this determination of faith, I went to Sharon's room and talked with her about the Biblical references to the laying on of hands for healing. I remember saying to her, "Sharon, I want you to believe that these are not just my hands. According to the Lord's promise to live in each true believer, these are the Lord's hands." I prayed with confidence that my God, who had answered so many prayers, would not fail us now.

It was not a gradual recovery, but an instantaneous change! Her strength returned. Her appetite improved. The symptoms disappeared, including the itching and the pains. Sharon was well immediately! The symptoms never returned, and we were on our way to the Kogis.

Since I had to return to Bogota, the capital of Colombia, for some necessary paper work, I arranged with Russell to fly Patty and Sharon to the north coast, planning to meet them at Cienaga, our shuttle point at the base of the mountains.

The graceful blue and white Cessna 182 climbed unfalteringly over the 11,000-foot ridge of the Andes and emerged over the savanna of Bogota, a broad plateau more than 8,000 feet above sea level, on which the capital of Colombia is built. Covering Russell's straight blond hair was a cap with gold lettering that read *Capitán Martín*. Since the name, Russell, is quite unpronounceable in Spanish, he used his middle name, Martin, in Latin America. All pilots are respectfully given the title of captain in Colombia.

Sharon and Patty settled themselves for the five-hour flight. Crammed into the backseat with Sharon were the boxes of medicine and other supplies. Sharon's slender, jean-clad figure and piquant face belied her twenty-four years. People usually took her for a teenager rather than the competent nurse that she really was.

They landed just outside the town of Cienaga, expecting to find me waiting for them, but no one had seen me. They registered at a hotel nearby, and arose early the next morning, hoping to find me at the Cienaga airstrip. But no luck! No one had seen me. They sadly climbed into the Cessna and headed for the mountains.

As they sped towards the little landing strip tucked away in the mountains, Patty felt a twinge of apprehension. How she wished that I were on board. In our family I was the one who usually made the decisions and handled the emergencies. What would they do if they found guerrillas in Mamarongo? How would they handle the care of the many sick Kogis? As Patty analyzed the situation, she came to the conclusion that there was just one thing to do: commit their safety to God. It was up to Him to protect them and to give them wisdom in treating the sick. They would go forward in faith and face the problems one at a time.

They were now in a narrow canyon, formed by a swift, crystalline river, one of those which drains the melting snow and heavy rainfall from the Sierra. Born in icy lakes, high above the tree line, these turbulent mountain streams rush their way from some 19,000 feet to sea level in less than forty miles—white-water all the way. As the Cessna progressed up the canyon, the rectangular, tin-roofed buildings of the Latin coffee growers soon gave way to the round, thatch-roofed dwellings of the Kogi Indians, perched high on the ridges. Patty and Sharon, watching from the windows, saw small white-clad figures emerge from the huts to gaze at the incoming airplane.

Two rivers, coming together in a V, had formed a long, narrow strip of level land. It had been freed of rocks and its grassy surface now resembled a small airstrip. At one end stood a cluster of simple, round structures whose woven cane walls and peaked thatched roofs manifested the handiwork of the Kogis. Off to the right stood several rectangular buildings and a simple, aluminum-roofed A-frame house.

After many years of living in a mud-walled dwelling, built for us by the Indians, I had asked permission to build the A-frame. Knowing that they did not want a "white man's building" in their territory, I assured them that this was another kind of Indian house, a wigwam. The Kogis had readily given permission and seemed quite pleased with it.

As the plane circled overhead, someone on the ground started a smudge fire to indicate wind conditions. The airstrip appeared like a small postage stamp in the steep valley below. Russell's body tensed in extreme concentration, as he made the final turn. There would be only one chance. On this strip there was no go-around. Patty and Sharon were silently praying as the Cessna settled onto the strip. A group of Kogis in their typical hand-woven white clothing quickly gathered to welcome them. Salomon and Amanda, a Latin couple who have been our co-workers in Mamarongo for many years, soon joined the group and reported that they knew of no new developments of guerrilla activity in the area.

"You better go sleep with an Indian family," Russell advised Patty just as he was getting into the plane. Apparently, he was a little worried about leaving his mother and sister there. "It will be safer than sleeping in the A-frame in case the guerrillas heard the airplane and arrive to kidnap a *gringo*.[1]

"I'll stop at Cienaga to see if Dad is there," he promised Patty as he got into the plane. "If he's not, I'll head straight back to San Martin; the plane is due for a mandatory government inspection there tomorrow."

It is always a bit disconcerting to stand on the edge of the tiny airstrip and watch the airplane whizz down the runway, pull up at the end, and soar away down the canyon, becoming smaller and smaller, until it is just a speck in the blue sky and white clouds. It is our best contact with the outside world. The alternative is to descend an eight-hour trail, slogging through the mud, to arrive at the frontier town of Palmor, from which it may be possible to catch a ride in a four-wheel-drive vehicle for the hazardous journey down the narrow, twisting mountain road to Cienaga.

This time, as the plane gathered momentum and lifted up into the air, Patty's thoughts returned to me. Why hadn't I shown up? The fact of the matter was: I simply had no way to inform Patty that the paperwork in Bogota took longer than I had anticipated. By the time I arrived in Cienaga, Russell had just left.

I couldn't believe it! Now I would have to hike over the trail, right through the area where the guerrillas were active. This trail was noted for killings and robberies in the best of times, and now with the Marxist guerrillas in the area, it seemed suicidal. The trauma of the guerrillas firing at my plane was still fresh in my mind. I was scared.

I returned to Santa Marta and spent three days in prayer, enlisting the prayer support of friends who were veteran mis-

---

[1]*gringo*—once a derogatory term for people from the United States, it has now lost much of its negative connotation in Colombia.

sionaries. We prayed until I was sure the Lord wanted me to take such a risk as hiking in would entail. My presence in Palmor, the town where the trail begins, and my passing along the trail past coffee farms would alert everyone who saw me that I was in the tribal area. It seemed very probable that the guerrillas would soon be informed.

As I prayed, I was greatly troubled as to why I had missed our plane at Cienaga. Feeling certain that God wanted me in the Kogi area to help during this devastating epidemic, I couldn't figure out why He allowed me to miss such a vital connection.

I later recalled that it was the papers for an importation that had delayed me.

According to the customs of Colombia, I had paid an agent to have the papers expedited, and he utilized a way that was a little dubious. No wonder the Lord didn't bless my connections that day.

I had to pay the consequences of this unwise act, and at five o'clock in the morning, the next day after I felt peace about undertaking this trip, I was bumping up the terrible road toward Mamarongo in a four-wheel-drive jeep, huddled in the back with other passengers and freight.

Patty crosses river to treat sick Kogi woman.

CHAPTER 4

Armed Intruders

Sierra Nevada de Santa Marta

Patty and Sharon did not have much time to contemplate the situation. Even before the airplane was out of sight, the sick began arriving. They had left their little thatched-roofed shelters the moment they had heard the airplane motor in the distance.

Sharon organized her medicines in a corner of Amanda's mud-walled kitchen. Expertly, she sorted out the patients, treating the most serious cases first. To her surprise she was able to communicate somewhat in the Kogi language. Out of her memory came long-forgotten phrases, learned when she was ten or twelve years old and spent her school vacations in the tribe.

"If I don't think, but just speak, I can do it," she confided to Patty, as their paths crossed in the kitchen. "I can just hear my doctors prescribing for these people in my mind," she added. Sharon had spent a year working in a government bilingual clinic in Florida.

While Sharon managed the medical work, Patty tackled another area of tribal need. Of the missionaries ministering in the area, she was the only one who had learned to extract teeth. After suffering with several severe toothaches in remote places far from dental services, Patty let compassion overcome her fastidiousness and learned to pull teeth. Several dentist friends provided her with the necessary equipment and basic instruction. Now she was deluged with Kogis who were determined to be relieved of their aching teeth.

By nightfall Patty and Sharon were too exhausted to even think about going up the side of the mountain to sleep in one of the Indians' houses. They made up beds on the second floor of the A-frame house that the boys and I had built of hand-sawn lumber, not far from the building that housed Amanda's kitchen.

Some of the sick were too ill to come for treatment, so Sharon arranged to have medicine taken to them by family members. One of these was an elderly woman who was gravely ill. Her daughter had died of the same illness just three days before Patty and Sharon arrived. Sharon told the relatives to keep her advised of the condition of these seriously sick Kogis and promised to visit them as soon as she could.

Three days later, the stream of patients slowed down, and Patty and Sharon turned their attention to other things, such as unpacking, worrying about the guerrillas and my whereabouts.

They asked the Kogis if they had seen any subversives, but it was very difficult for the Indians to distinguish between guerrillas and the army. To them, all non-Indians with uniforms and guns were suspect.

The next Saturday Sharon and Patty started hearing rumors that a group of men was on their way from Palmor. Some thought they were the guerrillas; others thought they were the police or the army. About eight o'clock that evening they saw lights coming down the trail and prepared themselves for an encounter with unknown visitors, but it was only the two sons of the head-man of the village who had been sent by their father to tell them that an army patrol was on the way. They were also told that a young Kogi woman, Mariana, who was like a daughter to Patty, had been commandeered to carry the lieutenant's backpack. The patrol could arrive at any moment.

As the brothers were sipping their hot coffee, Mariana herself arrived, breathless and excited. She had outdistanced the soldiers, left the lieutenant's pack in a house in the village, and was rushing to her home some twenty minutes farther on down the trail to warn her family to hide the shotguns and any other valuables. (The army and police had the reputation of appropriating any weapons they found.) Mariana had taken time to stop at our house and warn Patty and Sharon, too.

They waited and waited, but no one showed up. Finally they went to bed but jolted awake every time the dogs barked. In the morning everything seemed normal. Patty prepared a large kettle of coffee, sweetened with *panela*, the local brown sugar, so as to be ready to extend hospitality to any visitor.

About ten o'clock that morning, up the airstrip came a line of soldiers. Amazingly, Francisco Gil, Mariana's father, marched at the head of the column, his long, black hair and loose-fitting Kogi tunic flapping in the breeze. Straight to the back door of Amanda's kitchen Francisco marched with the soldiers behind him. With a desperate look on his face, as if to say, 'Please don't blame me, I couldn't help it,' he stood mutely in the doorway.

A young lieutenant brushed Francisco aside and introduced himself. "Are you the wife of Chad Stendal?" he asked. Patty was surprised, but realized that I must have checked in with the authorities in Santa Marta so she answered in the affirmative.

"He told us you were here," continued the lieutenant. "Why was Francisco so reluctant to bring us here?"

Patty replied that she didn't know, but later, talking with Francisco, she discovered that he had been sure that these men must be the dreaded guerrillas about whom Patty and Sharon had been inquiring. He had tried his best to bypass our house, but the lieutenant had insisted on being taken there. Poor Francisco, he was afraid that he had betrayed Patty and Sharon into the hands of the enemy.

The soldiers spread themselves on the ground between the A-frame and the kitchen and started removing their boots. Their leather army boots and socks had been drenched for two days, and their feet were in deplorable condition. Patty found a can of foot powder, which was gratefully accepted and passed around.

Patty offered coffee, but her act of hospitality was declined. This was surprising, as it was the first time in her nineteen years in Colombia, that anyone in the Sierra Nevada had turned down a cup of *tinto*. One soldier placed a huge kettle of water over the hole in the middle of Amanda's iron stoveplate,

Chad and Kogi friend prepare for a trip.

cutting off the draft and thus smothering the fire. He informed Patty that he was the cook and that the troops had not yet had breakfast. He planned on giving them each a cup of hot chocolate if he could get the kettle to boil.

Sharon struck up a conversation with the lieutenant who claimed to be only twenty-two years old. She discovered that they were under orders to refuse proffered food and beverages for fear of being poisoned by the local populace, some of whom were considered to be under the influence of the guerrillas.

Francisco had accepted a *tinto* and sat on a bench in the patio, keeping an eye on the soldiers as he emptied his cup. Realizing that the Kogi suffered no ill effects, the lieutenant and his three non-commissioned officers overcame their reluctance and relaxed on the wooden benches, and enjoyed a cup of our own mountain-grown brew.

At the arrival of the soldiers, several visiting Kogis had faded into the background, but now they too came forward, and those who could communicate a bit in Spanish conversed with the soldiers. Meanwhile, the army cook vainly fanned the fire under his huge kettle of water.

Amanda returned from the stream where she had been doing her laundry, and after her initial shock at the invasion of her kitchen, she revived the fire and expertly brought the kettle to a boil. She tactfully suggested that the young cook build his own fire outside. The sergeant purchased two chickens from our closest Kogi neighbor, and the cook proceeded to make a watery soup with the chicken and some green bananas donated by Amanda.

"You are living very dangerously," the lieutenant told Sharon. "You are as exposed as actors on a stage in this open valley, as you go back and forth between the A-frame and the kitchen. If you have to be up here, you should go and sleep in the Indian houses where you would not be so visible."

While Sharon conversed with the lieutenant, Patty made friends with the three non-coms. The two corporals claimed to be twenty-two years old, the same as the lieutenant, while the sergeant, the old man of the group, declared himself to be twenty-five. The enlisted men were all nineteen years of age and were mostly from the same small town in the department of Antioquia. They had only two months left of their eighteen month tour of duty. Their only desire was to stay out of the hands of the guerrillas for those two months, then return to civilian life.

The officers, who were all making the army their career, interrogated the visiting Indians about guerrilla activity in the area, but without much success. They tried to explain to the

Chad in Kogi clothes talks with a Kogi chief.

Kogis that the soldiers were the good people, but that there were also bad people running around the mountains. They pointed out the distinguishing features: The army wears uniforms, but the guerrillas wear parts of uniforms mixed with civilian clothing. The army sleeps in the night and moves around in the daytime, while the guerrillas hole up during the day and move at night. "Like jaguars," commented one Kogi.

The most distinctive feature of the guerrillas, which really impressed the Kogis as being odd, was the fact that women are incorporated into the ranks of the guerrillas, while the army consists of men only. The sergeant admonished the Kogis to inform the soldiers immediately should they know anything about the whereabouts of the guerrillas.

"What will you do if you do catch some of the guerrillas?" Patty innocently asked the sergeant.

She was not prepared for the dark look of hatred that crossed his young face. "Those people are rotten to the core," he exclaimed with emotion, thrusting his forefinger significantly at his jugular vein, "They must not be allowed to live."

By suppertime the soldiers had lost all fear of being poisoned and very willingly consumed any leftovers, coming right into the kitchen and scraping out the cooking kettles. As darkness fell, the lieutenant entered the kitchen, and after a few terse words, all the army personnel disappeared. They set up their camp at the far end of the airstrip. The lieutenant returned alone after a while to chat around the dying embers of the campfire.

In the morning after a meager breakfast, the visitors faded off into the underbrush, only the officers stopping to say goodbye.

After the soldiers had disappeared, Patty and Sharon wondered what they should do. It was likely that the next visitors would be the guerrillas. They decided to take the lieutenant's advice and go to live with the Indians.

Providentially, the son of the old Kogi woman, who was the most seriously ill of all their patients, showed up to report on his mother's condition. She was not doing well. She was still in her hammock and was not eating. The young man, Vicente, was rather startled to learn that the missionaries were going home with him, and that they were going to stay all night. He was even more astounded when they handed him a duffel bag containing hammocks and sleeping bags and asked him to carry it. Most Kogis are proud of their ability to carry heavy burdens by a head-strap, and the duffel was not very heavy, however Vicente was his mother's last child, born when she was middle-aged, and had been a skinny, yellow-faced little fellow with toothpick legs when we had first come to Mamarongo. We had probably saved his life many times over with powdered milk, vitamins, and parasite treatments. He was the Kogi version of the pampered youngest child.

With much complaining he was finally persuaded to carry the duffel bag. Sharon and Patty came behind with *mochilas*, Kogi carrying bags, over their shoulders, containing medicines and personal items. They found the old woman lying quietly in her hammock. The elderly and sick among the Kogis are as likely to die of starvation as of whatever disease they might have. Nursing care is unknown among them. Unless a Kogi gets up at mealtime and takes his place around the family cooking pot, he is apt to go without.

As soon as the old grandmother saw Patty, a smile lit up her face. She knew now that she would get better. Some good nourishing food (oatmeal and powdered milk), and some tender, loving care were all she needed.

At the same time that Patty and Sharon were with the Indians, I arrived in Palmor. I got out of the jeep and walked through the streets of Palmor, a frontier town of about 3,000 people. I had an old hat pulled down over my blond hair and old clothes, trying to look like a local country person. Fortunately it seemed to work, and nobody seemed to pay much attention to me. I knew where the trail started, and soon I was bounding quickly along the mountain trail. Since no one knew I was coming, no one from Mamarongo met me with mules. I was all alone, moving as quickly as possible, since I wanted to outdistance anyone starting after me from town. I also knew side trails and short cuts that I could make on foot, avoiding parts of the main mule trail. I had gotten this far, and I did not intend to be ambushed or caught from behind. After eight hours of steep, uphill climb, and after fording several rivers, I saw the airstrip and our A-frame. I studied the area carefully, but everything seemed peaceful.

By the next morning Patty noted with satisfaction that the old Kogi grandmother was significantly better, having responded to the combined treatment of prayer, medicine, food, and love. Once more Patty and Sharon questioned the Kogis about guerrilla activity, but it was clear that they could not distinguish between the army and the subversives. The women decided to leave their belongings there and go back to the A-frame for a bath and change of clothes. When they wearily trudged into Amanda's kitchen, a surprise was waiting for them.

Their long-lost husband and father had arrived.

The first landing in Mamarongo.

CHAPTER 5

Capitalism/Communism/ Christianity

April 1983

In spite of the lieutenant's warning, I decided we should stay at the A-frame. People were still arriving every day for medical treatment, and it was a disappointment for them to find us gone. Also, our main supply of medicine was there at the airstrip. I set up a plan of escape in case the guerrillas arrived.

The land upon which our house is built is owned by Alfonso, a Kogi who grew up in our family. He now lives in another part of the Sierra, and Salomon and Amanda run a small coffee plantation for him, sometimes employing Latin laborers. The coffee harvest was coming to an end. The next Thursday the last of the coffee berries were picked in the morning, and the two workers, young men in their mid-twenties, entered into a conversation with Sharon and Patty around the dinner table at noon. I had left early that morning to check on the old woman and visit some of the other Kogis who were recovering from the epidemic upriver from the airstrip. The talk turned to the visit of the soldiers, and it was obvious that at least one man was not kindly disposed towards the military, even though he had served a tour of duty in the army.

"It is inevitable that the Communists eventually will take over the country," he calmly stated, toying with his empty coffee cup. When Sharon and Patty recovered from their shock, they asked why it was inevitable.

"Because it is obvious that a change in government is needed," the coffee picker firmly stated. He went on to describe the low moral character of the country as a whole: law enforcement agents who encouraged bribes, politicians who used money designated for highways and public works to line their own pockets, tremendous unemployment, starvation wages for common laborers.

"Capitalism has failed," he finally declared. "We need a change, and the only alternative on the horizon is Communism. We will have to give it a try."

Sharon at once rose to the challenge. "What makes you think things will be any better under Communism?" she asked. "As long as people are selfish and dishonest, no form of government will bring peace and prosperity. What is needed is not a change in the form of government, but a change of heart. Unless the leaders of a nation are men of integrity, social conditions are not going to get better. The hope for Colombia and for the world is a wide-spread turning to God. When people give up their own selfishness and begin to be motivated by a spirit of love and good-will towards others, then we will see an end to the abuses and social problems that exist."

The afternoon wore on. The coffee pickers did not leave the table, and neither did Sharon and Patty. More coffee was served and the debate continued.

Francisco, Chad and two coffee pickers prepare for trip.

"It is not the form of government that causes the problem," Patty continued. "Capitalism is only as good as the moral quality of the population of the nation. It is only as individual people come to God in repentance for their sin and selfishness and allow Him to forgive them, turn their lives around, and empower them to live a life of love, integrity, and unselfishness, that we can see a change for the better."

I entered just as Amanda started putting supper on the table. One of the coffee pickers turned to me. He was the man who had expected a Communist take-over.

"Could we have a worship service tonight?" he asked.

Salomon and Amanda readily agreed, and as soon as the supper dishes were cleared away, out came Bibles and hymn books. After a time of singing, led by Salomon with his rich, bass voice, a passage of Scripture was read, and I expounded its meaning. Everyone felt free to contribute ideas or interject questions. After a short time of prayer, the meeting was dismissed.

"Can we do this again tomorrow night?" the coffee pickers asked. It would be their last night in Mamarongo. The next evening both men told us that they could now see a better solution to the problems in Colombia, and they both opened their hearts to God's transforming grace.

"That one man was really a guerrilla sympathizer," Patty remarked after they had left. "But it was amazing how quickly he turned his heart to God, once he understood the true message of the Gospel."

"I know," replied Sharon. "I'm not going to worry about being kidnapped anymore. If the Communists get me, I will know it is because God needs a witness among the guerrillas."

The weeks sped by. The epidemic was nearing the end, but some patients were still coming to us each day for treatment. No one had died since our arrival. Sharon decided to stay another month to oversee the care of the Kogis who were still recovering.

Patty and I left Mamarongo to prepare for traveling to the United States, where I had speaking engagements. I left immediately for Minnesota, and Patty went out to Chaparral to visit Chaddy and show Gospel movies in the *llanos*. A few weeks later she joined me but brought distressing news. Rickey Kirby had been kidnapped. She had been tied up and taken away in her own Toyota. The guerrillas had been waiting for her when she came in from riding her range. They took away Tom's crutches and left him alone and helpless, so that he couldn't put the authorities immediately on their trail. Upon being discovered, he had been taken to a hospital in Villavicencio, the capital of the *llanos*, where he was in poor condition. The governor had gone on the radio, requesting her release so that she could be with her critically ill husband, but the kidnappers were silent.

We were all deeply saddened by this news. We spent much time praying for Rickey and wondering what might be happening to her. Chaddy said he would try to rescue her if he could find out where she was being held, but no one knew. Squatters moved in on the Kirby land, and some of their cattle disappeared. Friends of the Kirbys from Villavicencio were able to secure some of the cattle and sold the ranch house. Tom, grieving in his hospital bed, decided Rickey's heart had not been equal to the strain and assumed that she had probably died soon after her capture.

About this time Russell decided to give up his work as a jungle pilot. He told us he was selling the Cessna 182 and moving to Bogota. He and his Colombian friend, Ricardo Trillos, were engaged in a ministry of family reconciliation based on the Sermon on the Mount. They had seen amazing results in repairing broken family relationships, and now Russell would be working full time in this ministry. He would try to sell the fish business. He was very concerned about Rickey Kirby and vowed to do all in his power to locate her and secure her release.

Chad, Pat, Russell, Chaddy, Gloria, Marina and Sharon.

CHAPTER 6

Let's Get This Show on the Road

August, 1983, Bogota and San Martin

Patty and I returned to Colombia, accompanied by our youngest daughter, Gloria, who had just completed high school in Minnesota. Russell met us in Bogota. He had been having a hard time financially since he had quit flying in the jungle and looked pale and thin.

He proudly showed us his apartment. His Colombian wife, Marina, and baby daughter, Lisa, were awaiting our return to San Martin, so that they could move permanently to Bogota. About half of their belongings had been moved, and the other half was still in San Martin.

I questioned him about his source of income, and it seemed that he had lived the last few months by selling junk and unneeded items, both his and mine, out of our home in San Martin. He was looking forward to living in Bogota, working with his Colombian friends in an effort to counsel and strengthen families, reconciling husbands with wives and parents with children.

A few months before, Russell and Ricardo had received tremendous insights on the Sermon on the Mount. Russell had arrived in Minnesota just before the Good Friday service in a Grand Rapids church. Although I was to bring the message, the pastor wanted to introduce Russell and have him bring a greeting. "How much time do you think your son would take?" he had asked me.

"Well, if he speaks five minutes, it will be four more than he's ever spoken before," I replied.

Russell was duly introduced and spoke effectively with great power for some forty-five minutes. He saw that the Sermon on the Mount was not just applicable in some future kingdom age but was the Lord's direction for living the Christian life today. He also saw that the Beatitudes built on one another and were not just unconnected sayings, and that the teaching about the man who built his house (household) upon the rock had a clear application to applying the Sermon on the Mount to the family.[1]

I had been astounded. It seemed that along with the message, he had received the gift and power to communicate it effectively. Patty and I were discussing whether Russell's ministry was needed the most here in Colombia, or in North America. We couldn't decide.

Patty presented him with a gift, a new bright blue *Capitán Martín* cap with gold braid and large, gold letters. We expected him to be delighted, as the old one was now worn and faded, but to our surprise, he just looked at it pensively and remarked, "I don't really think I should be wearing something like this— too conspicuous, with so much terrorism occurring."

He sat down in a chair with a sigh. "Don't you like this apartment, Dad, I feel so *safe* here."

A guard tower stood at the entrance to the apartment complex. Several armed, uniformed men patrolled the grounds and challenged strangers at the entrance. Russell had traded his Cessna 182 for the apartment. Now we would have to use the smaller, lower-powered Cessna 170 for all our flights, however it would be adequate now that Russell had given up commercial flying.

In a few days Patty and I traveled to San Martin. We planned to spend a few weeks there before returning to Mamarongo. Marina and Russell were preparing for their final move to Bogota. Nine-month-old Lisa was a delight. She had just started walking, and Russell was tremendously proud of her. They played airplane every night just before bedtime, as

---

[1]See Appendix A.

Russell whirled her around by an arm and a leg while she made airplane noises.

Russell had now decided to leave the *llanos*, feeling the call to the ministry in Bogota. He felt that we should all withdraw from eastern Colombia before we lost everything, including our lives, to the advancing tide of Communism.

We asked Russell how Chaddy was getting along out in Chaparral. Russell replied that he felt that Chaparral had outlived its usefulness, and he wanted to see everything sold, and the proceeds used to further the other ministries in which we were involved. But Chaddy refused to budge. My two sons were as different as night and day. Chaddy was possessive and tenacious, while Russell was quick to move on to new things. Their personalities were so dissimilar, that from early childhood there had been friction between them. Chaddy was most emphatic that we must not back down and leave, no matter what the threat.

I encouraged Russell to make one last trip to the ranch in support of Chaddy, before he left the *llanos*. Almost immediately I had to return to Bogota. I was working on the paperwork that was so necessary to keep the airplane license and our visas and passports current.

Saturday evening Russell was preparing for an early morning flight, his last one into the jungle. Marina was not in favor of the flight. She had heard rumors that caused her to advise Russell to stay out of the jungle. At the supper table Patty encouraged Russell to start work on a book he was contemplating, telling about his life and the message of the Sermon on the Mount. "I can't get it to come together," Russell replied. "I can't see how to structure the book. I need just the right experience to illustrate the message."

Russell would stop at Chaparral, and Patty was preparing some packages of used clothing for some of the needy families in the area. "Mother, we have to get Chaddy out of there. The place is going haywire," Russell remarked. Patty wrote a letter to Chaddy, asking him to come back with Russell to San Martin, and possibly go to the Kogi area with us.

"What do you know about Rickey Kirby?" Patty asked Russell.

"Nothing," he replied. "It's been four months now, and

there's no word about her. I've asked everywhere possible and haven't been able to pick up a thing."

Russell and Patty discussed the political and spiritual situation of the country. It seemed that a crisis was developing. They agreed that a major spiritual renewal was needed to save the country, beginning with our family. "I don't know about the rest of the family, but I am willing to do whatever it takes to get this show on the road." With these words, Russell ended the conversation and went to bed.

The next day was Sunday, August 14. Russell took off early, and Marina and Lisa left to visit Marina's family. Gloria and her fiance, Uriel, accompanied Pat to the poorest section of town to hold Sunday services in various homes.

About four o'clock that afternoon, Patty was alone at home, waiting for Russell and Chaddy to return. As she finished some typing, she heard a car drive up and stop in front of the house. She rushed to the front window, expectantly hoping to see Chaddy alight from the jeep, but it was a small, white car at the gate, instead of the battered, red Toyota. Two strangers stood at the door with expressionless faces.

A stab of apprehension ran up Patty's spine. Since Rickey had been kidnapped, we were wary of strange visitors. However, these men looked kind, not as if they had sinister motives.

Finally the older one spoke. "Have you heard anything about a kidnapping?" he timidly asked.

"No," Patty replied. 'Strange that he should talk about a kidnapping right when I'm suspecting them,' Patty thought.

The man raised his eyes. They were incredibly sad. "There has been a kidnapping," he stated simply, but Patty interpreted it as a question.

"No, I know nothing about any kidnapping," she stated emphatically.

The man came quickly to the point. "There has been a kidnapping. Russell has been kidnapped!"

Patty's mind refused to accept the statement. This must be a mistake, something that they would be laughing about tomorrow. "How do you know?" she finally asked.

"I was Russell's companion on the flight this morning." Patty started to recognize Russell's friend, Gilberto. She had met him once or twice just before she went to the States.

The truth began to hit her. Our worst fears had been realized. RUSSELL HAD BEEN KIDNAPPED! Why didn't God protect him, like He had us in Mamarongo?

Gilberto was saying things like—"so very young . . . so very violent . . . Carlos tried to talk them out of it . . . almost killed, myself . . . a miracle I escaped . . . shooting submachine guns at our feet."

Then, like a flash of light to the innermost part of her heart, she heard God's voice.

> "This has happened for three reasons:
> (1) It will lead to the release of Mrs. Kirby.
> (2) It will result in spiritual-growth for
>   Chaddy and the rest of the family.
> (3) I need a witness among the Communist guerrillas."

A great peace took possession of Patty's emotions and mind. Gently, calmly, she said, "Please come in. Won't you sit down and tell me all about it."

A drug store on Main Street in Canyo Jabon. The sign in front offers the following goods and services: perfumes, application of injections and intervenous fluids, prescriptions filled, minor surgery, and first aid..

CHAPTER 7

Gilberto's Story

"First we landed at Mapiripan and delivered some mail to Russell's brother-in-law, Raul. Then we continued to Chaparral. Chaddy needed some supplies, and there was to be a town meeting in Canyo Jabon to consider the purchase of Russell's refrigeration equipment, so Russell invited me to join him in a short flight downriver to Canyo Jabon." Gilberto started his story, obviously ill-at-ease, sitting on the edge of his chair.

"Carlos, the president of the Canyo Jabon council, was waiting for us. The three of us walked down the road to Carlos' store, which is on the main street of town, close to the river.

"All of a sudden a group of young men, heavily armed, came running down the road. A shout went up that it was the army, but I sensed something sinister and knew that an unpleasant incident was about to happen.

"Russell disappeared inside the store. I almost followed him, but at the last minute decided to mix with some townspeople who were standing in the road. The newcomers roughly rounded us up into a group and told us to put our hands in the air.

"They were so young and so violent! They shot into the dust of the road right by our feet! I was sure we were going to he killed. They wore parts of army uniforms mixed with civilian clothes. They were only about sixteen or eighteen years old.

"The leader pointed his gun right at Carlos and ordered him to turn *Capitán Martín* over to him. I was sure they were going to kill Carlos. Finally Russell came out without the shotgun that he had been carrying. They ordered him to put his hands in the air and marched him away down the road towards the airstrip. That's the last I saw of him."

Gilberto put his face in his hands. He trembled all over as he relived his recent ordeal. Finally he pulled himself together, "I feel so bad to think of Russell being taken away all alone by those terrible, violent young men."

Patty felt a desire to comfort Gilberto. "Russell is not alone. God is with him," she assured him.

"I'm so glad you're taking it that way," Gilberto responded. "I hated to be the one to have to come and tell you this. I was afraid you would collapse, and we would have double trouble."

"When did this happen? How did you get back? Where is the airplane? Did the men identify themselves or say why they wanted Russell?" Patty's questions came tumbling out. Gilberto's companion, a tall, slender teenager, sat in shocked silence.

"I think it was about twelve thirty, just after noon. Some of the men wore armbands that said ELN.[1] Just before they disappeared from view, one of the gunmen shouted back, 'Tell the family that we want forty million pesos (half a million dollars), or they will never see him again.' " Once more Gilberto buried his head in his hands.

The huge amount of money they were asking was a further blow to Patty. The situation seemed hopeless. "What did you do then?" she asked.

"Before they left, one of the gunmen asked who was the person who came with Russell in the plane. I was terrified. I was sure they were going to shoot me. I just tried to make myself inconspicuous. No one pointed me out, and after a while they all went away. I stood around in the road for a while, along with some other people. Then I realized I had to figure out a way to get out of there, so after about half an hour I walked back to the airstrip.

"There were three planes on the ground—Russell's and two others belonging to German pilots. The planes had all been

---

[1]ELN stands for *Ejercito de Liberacion Nacional* (National Army of Liberation), a small subversive group that is active in central Colombia. The testimonies of the witnesses to Russell's kidnapping were confused; some reported seeing ELN armbands, while others reported that pamphlets left in town by the kidnappers bore EPL insignia. EPL stands for *Ejercito Popular de Liberacion* (Popular Army of Liberation), another a small subversive group, working in the more urban areas of Colombia and reportedly backed by Chinese Marxists.

damaged. They had been shot and chopped at with an axe. All the windshields were broken, and the microphones of all the radios had been taken. I reached into the back of Russell's plane for my small, blue suitcase, but it wasn't there.

"As I searched for my suitcase, one of the other pilots hollered at me to keep away from Russell's plane. I explained that I was the passenger who had flown into town with Russell. The pilot became very excited, 'You are really in danger here,' he told me. 'They have been asking all over for you. Here, get in my plane, and we will try to get out of here.'

"The nose cone had been chopped off his plane with an axe, but he threw the broken piece in the back of the plane and finished breaking the rest of the plexiglass out of the windshield. We took off, but it was terrible with the wind coming in. Soon after we took off, we heard shots being fired, and the door popped open. I tried to close the door, but it wouldn't close. The plane flew slowly and at an angle, but we managed to get to Mapiripan. I had to hold the door all the way. As we landed, I tried to shield the pilot's face from the wind with a piece of the broken plexiglass."

"When we landed," Gilberto continued, "We found the nose cone had wedged in the door, and that was why it wouldn't close. The pilot said it was a miracle. The open door made it possible for all the air that was coming in through the broken windshield to leave. Otherwise we couldn't have flown the plane.

"Raul was at the Mapiripan strip when we arrived. I told him what had happened, and he said he would get word to Chaddy at Chaparral. I also asked him to tell the police and try to contact you through a radio message to the police station here in San Martin. I was hoping I wouldn't have to be the one to tell you.

"Just after we landed, a commercial flight from Villavicencio came in. I was able to get passage to Villavo[2] and took the bus back to San Martin."

Gilberto looked drained after relating his story. His face was very white, and his arms and legs were trembling. After once again expressing his sympathy and offering the use of his telephone should we need it, Gilberto and his friend got into his small, white car and drove away.

---

[2]The local nickname for Villavicencio.

CHAPTER 8

Divine Comfort

After Gilberto had left, Patty tried to think what she should do. Russell had left the Toyota at the San Martin airstrip and the keys were in his pocket. She suddenly remembered that Fidel, the airplane mechanic, might have an extra set. He was terribly grieved to hear the bad news, but he did have a set of keys. He took off on his bicycle for the airstrip to bring back the jeep. Gloria and Uriel returned and went with Patty to tell Marina and her family the bad news. Of course, they were shocked and upset. Then Marina went with them to Gilberto's house to try to contact me in Bogota by telephone.

As Patty dialed, a crowd of neighbors gathered in Gilberto's living room to express sympathy and get in on the excitement. "Just call the American Embassy! They will give you the money to pay the ransom right away! They always do!" one of them advised. Patty frantically tried to tell them they were mistaken.

"Then call the Colombian government! They will have to give you the money because you are foreigners," someone else suggested. Patty couldn't believe their naivete. It was incredible that anyone would even think that we could come up with half a million dollars. The telephone connection to Bogota was not working. She dialed over and over again, trying every number she knew in Bogota. There was no phone in Russell's apartment where I was staying. Finally one call went through. It was the Hotel San Diego, where I usually stayed before Russell got the apartment. She asked them to call Russell's friend, Ricardo Trillos, and ask him to get word to me.

By this time the early, tropical night had fallen.[1] Patty and Marina returned home. They were exhausted, but sleep was impossible. Patty felt she must spend the night praying for Russell. She tried to imagine what might be happening to him. She wondered if they had killed him already. Were they torturing him? Was he hungry, wet, cold, or sick?

As the night wore on, rain started to fall. A damp chill permeated the room. "Oh God," Patty prayed. "Take care of Russell. Don't let them hurt him. Give him courage! Help him feel Your presence!"

She prayed for Chaddy and for Rickey Kirby too. She dozed, but awoke with a start and started praying again. It was still raining and unusually cold for the tropics.[2]

Finally she could stand it in the bedroom no longer. Taking her Bible, she went out to the dining room table in the cool, gray, misty pre-dawn light. A band of pain throbbed deep in her head behind her eyes. "Oh Lord," she prayed, "I'm never going to be able to take this! Why is this happening? Please give me a verse to stand on!"

As she waited quietly before the Lord, once again that still small voice spoke to her heart.

"I already gave you the verse! Don't you remember?"

Then she did remember. We had been traveling down through the southeastern states a few weeks before on our way back to Colombia. One night in a motel room she was awakened by a persistent thought—(Isaiah 41:10) . . . (Isaiah 41:10). She tried to shake it off and go back to sleep. (Isaiah 41:10). Finally she awakened sufficiently to realize that this was a verse she had memorized as a teenager.

> *Fear not for I am with you. Be not dismayed for I am your God. I will strengthen you, I will help you, I will uphold you with My victorious right hand.*

The next morning she had told me about it. We had been a little concerned about our safety as we returned to Colombia,

---

[1]Colombia, being on the Equator, has equal days and nights all year around. The sun comes up at 6:00 a.m, and goes down at 6:00 P.M. There is almost no twilight.
[2]Probably around 68°F.

and we had taken this verse as an encouragement from the Lord that He would protect us.

Now this morning, after receiving the terrible news about Russell, Patty opened her Bible and read the entire passage:

Behold, all who are incensed against you shall be put to shame and confounded; those who strive against you shall be as nothing and shall perish. You shall seek those who contend with you, but you shall not find them; those who war against you shall be as nothing at all. For I, the Lord your God, hold your right hand; it is I who say to you, Fear not I will help you.

Patty was astounded. It fit the situation so perfectly. She knew now that her words of comfort to Gilberto had not been empty. She thought, "God is with Russell! He is there in a very personal way. He is holding Russell's right hand." The heavy burden that was crushing her started to become bearable.

As Patty paged through the following chapters of Isaiah, several portions of verses lit up for her.

I will turn the darkness before them into light, the rough places into level ground. When you pass through the waters, I will be with you; through the rivers, they shall not overwhelm you; when you walk through fire you shall not be burned, and the flame shall not consume you.

It was getting light now. The air was still damp and heavy from the rain. Patty lay her tired head in her hands, elbows on the table. "Okay Lord," she sighed, "I know that Russell is in Your hands; that You are with him. I know that this kidnapping is a part of Your plan. It is going to result in Mrs. Kirby's release; in spiritual growth for Chaddy and all of us; and Russell is going to be a witness for You to the guerrillas. But please, if it's not too much to ask, please let me know right now if Russell is going to have to give his life. Don't give me any false hope just to make me feel better! Tell me the truth, right now! Don't try to soften the blow! I would rather know from the beginning. Will we get Russell back again? Or will the end of this matter be that he will go to be with You?"

Her prayer had been from the heart, as sincere as she knew how to make it. She waited quietly before God for a few minutes; then continued slowly paging through Isaiah, her heavy eyes skimming the columns of print. All of a sudden a verse leaped out of the page and into her heart.

He who is bowed down shall speedily be released; He shall not die and go down to the pit, Neither shall his bread fail." (Isaiah 51:14)

It could not have been clearer: Russell was not going to die, he would be released! Patty was also reassured that he would not go hungry.

A few minutes later Marina came out of her bedroom. One look at her face told Patty that her night had been no better than hers. As a matter of fact, it had been worse. In addition to her own grief and sense of loss, little Lisa had cried for her father off and on all night. Of course the baby did not understand what had happened, but she missed her daddy and her nightly simulated "airplane ride." Every time she woke up through the night and saw his empty place in the bed, she sobbed.

Russell had married three years before, while all the rest of the family were in the United States.[3] We had not known Marina before her marriage to Russell. Russell had warned us not to try to "evangelize" Marina. She and her family had experienced some unfortunate incidents with *evangelicos* as Protestants are called in Colombia. They preferred their Catholic faith. Russell assured us that he would take the responsibility for the well-being of Marina's soul. Since we knew that he walked close to God (at least most of the time), we had to accept the situation. Patty had come to love Marina as a person and as a daughter-in-law but had never talked with her, heart to heart, about spiritual things. Now, after three years, a barrier had built up.

One look at Marina's woebegone face broke Patty's heart. Marina had passed through the dining room and gone into the kitchen to get a cold drink from the refrigerator. 'How can I keep this good news to myself?' Patty thought. Yet how could she expect Marina to believe this story of God talking to her?

---

[3]The story of Russell and Marina's marriage is told in *Rescue the Captors* by Russell Stendal, Ransom Press International, P.O. Box 1456, Burnsville, MN 55337.

Of Scripture verses in the middle of the night? Of God's voice talking to her at the door while Gilberto was telling the bad news? Bible verses jumping off the page? It would be impossible for her to understand. She would think Patty was "cracking up." But how could Patty keep this good news to herself? It had to be shared.

"Marina, come here and sit down a minute!" Patty called. "I have something to tell you."

CHAPTER 9

Call Out the Heavy Artillery

August 15, 1983

The next day in Bogota, I was called to the phone to receive a call from my good friend, Ricardo. I noticed that he didn't greet me with his usual boisterous style. He talked very slowly and sadly, and I knew something was wrong. Then he told me, "Your son, Russell, has been kidnapped in the jungle at Canyo Jabon."

I couldn't believe it, and I questioned him thoroughly. Finally he said, "I'm very sorry, Chad, but it is true". I was stunned, but I still thought that there might be some mistake.

During many years of hazardous jungle and mountain flying, Russell had been erroneously reported killed or crashed a number of times. One time a woman appeared at our door, all dressed in black to bring us the news that she had heard that Russell's plane had crashed, and he had been killed. Several times his plane had been overdue, sometimes for days, but he always turned up. Once when he was overdue, another plane had crashed in the area where he was flying, and everyone was sure it was Russell. The next day the little Cessna appeared out of the blue. He appeared to have a charmed life. As a matter fact, I believe the Lord had protected him through a whole series of close calls.

This time, however, it was different. As I returned rapidly to San Martin and talked to the eyewitnesses of the kidnapping, it became very certain that he was, indeed, in guerrilla hands. The guerrilla band had identified themselves as the EPL or Popular Liberation Army. My heart sank because this group had the worst reputation for ruthless killing. It seemed very likely that they would torture him for information and then kill him, since they often consider any American in a rural area as a spy and member of the CIA.

I couldn't understand why Russell had made no attempt to escape. Chaddy, Russell, and I had talked it all over one day and agreed that in the event of being kidnapped, the best thing to do would be to escape. Both boys were at home in the jungle, and if anyone could survive and find their way back to civilization it would be my sons. It seemed that he could have dived into the river from the back door of Carlos' house. I also wondered why he didn't fire the shotgun. If he were still alive and not injured, I expected him to make an attempt to get away.

Knowing that prayer is the Christian's best weapon, now that we were engaged in such a battle for Russell's life, we felt that we needed to call out all the "high-powered equipment." The guerrillas were well-armed with submachine guns and automatic weapons, but we had access to God's heavy artillery.

As soon as I ascertained the facts of the situation, I sat down and wrote a letter to the folks back home.

San Martin, Colombia
August 16, 1983

Dear Friends,

The violence in Colombia is such that I often stated when speaking in the U.S. that our family would not be able to make it through this year without one of us being killed, wounded, or kidnapped, unless God intervened. Yet I felt the Lord would have us stay in Colombia. I have felt great spiritual concern for the idealistic guerrillas who believe they are the salvation of Colombia, but who actually are causing great destruction. I tried to think of ways of witnessing to them, but they live in such seclusion that it seemed impossible. Well, God has sent them a missionary.

YESTERDAY, MY SON, RUSSELL, WAS KIDNAPPED by a subversive group sponsored by the Chinese Communists but is considered much more fanatical and blood-thirsty than the Russian-Cuban Communists.

We would very much appreciate your prayers. Tonight I know that Russell is talking to the guerrillas about the Lord and the change that can come into their lives through Him. I also know that we serve a God who fully understands what it means to a father when his son is in the hands of ruthless men.

Sincerely in Christ,
Chad Stendal and family

The telephone line to San Martin was now completely out of order. Airmail service had recently been discontinued. Even the telegraph system was not functioning. Some of us sped to Villavicencio to alert our prayer warriors. Patty sent a telegram to her sister and brother-in-law in Minnesota: RUSSELL KIDNAPPED PRAY COMMUNICATE. Gloria and Uriel helped Patty to get sixty of my letters in the mail before the post office closed, using the gummed labels intended for our Christmas cards. Back at San Martin, we all worked until late that night getting some two hundred more letters prepared for mailing. Patty was obsessed with getting letters out. She wanted the whole world to know what these terrible people had done in taking Russell. She thought that if overwhelming public opinion was rallied against their atrocious act, they would see that they were doing their cause no good and release our son. She felt her job was to rally recruits to stand with us in the prayer battle that had just begun.

Those first few days Patty kept reading us Bible verses which she said God was bringing to her attention. They all pointed to the fact that God was strengthening Russell, giving him courage, and using him as a witness to his captors.

Marina handled her grief well. Her long, solemn face gave the only indication of her inner pain. Marina is a very private person and was not yet ready to share her grief with the outside world. She felt that any publicity jeopardized Russell's chances.

Meanwhile, in Minneapolis, the telegram arrived. Sharon happened to be at her aunt's house when it came, and she made immediate plans to join us. By "communicate" Patty had meant that they should tell people to pray, but our brother-in-law, Ralph Burton, called the news media. The story circled the globe. It was headline news in Minnesota. Patty's sister, Dorothe, appeared on television. My elderly father was also filmed in his home in Florida. Soon the American Embassy in Bogota was swamped with calls for information; but no additional information was available to the Embassy or the news-hungry journalists. At San Martin we were still completely isolated from the outside world.

I was wracking my brain for ideas. Where should we search? Who might be able to help? We were faced with the major problem of getting the airplane repaired and out of Canyo Jabon before it would be stripped down and carried off in pieces by the local people. Even though the guerrilla band that kidnapped Russell had left, there would be other guerrillas and sympathizers in the area. There were no government police or army units there, so anything we tried to do would be exceedingly dangerous. However, without the plane, we would be greatly hampered in our search for Russell, and later on our Kogi Indian work would be greatly impeded. After much prayer, I decided we would have to rescue the airplane.

I was overwhelmed by agonizing grief. The conclusion to which my logical thinking led me was that Russell was probably already dead. I knew he carried Civil Air Patrol identification that could lead the guerrillas to believe he was a government agent. I searched through all his drawers and papers, hoping to find this I.D. card but without success. My only hope was that he had had sufficient presence of mind to hide it in Carlos' store or get rid of it somehow.

On Wednesday evening, three days after Russell had been captured, Hernan, one of Marina's brothers arrived with a letter from Chaddy.

Chaparral
August 15, 1983

Hello Mom and Dad,

First of all remember that God is in charge of all things. Please don't worry! I'm fine and will have Russ back (with God's help) in a few days.

I almost ground looped the plane on take-off when the windshield exploded. (It had been busted with an axe.) If you will come down and fly it back to San Martin, it would be better. Mechanically it is fine. No windshield and no left door are the problems. (It flies sideways.) Russ was taken yesterday by the ELN. They are asking forty million pesos. I offered 500,000.

Russ might be O.K. He wasn't searched very good, and his revolver wasn't found. He had a leg holster.[1]

---

[1]In Colombia pilots are supposed to carry a gun as a survival tool in case of airplane crash. Russell carried a pistol in a leg holster. The story of the consequences of carrying this pistol is told in *Rescue the Captors*.

If you come down, come straight to Chaparral. If either police or military come to Canyo Jabon, I'm afraid they will impound the airplane. (It would be good to get the plane out as soon as possible.) Maybe Fidel could come and install a new windshield. Here at Chaparral I don't think you would be taking any risk.

DON'T FORGET TO LET GOD SOLVE ALL PROBLEMS!

> With love,
> Chaddy

The tension was broken. For the first time since Russell was kidnapped, we could relax and smile a little. Good ole Chaddy would figure it out.

Hernan had accompanied Chaddy to Canyo Jabon. He told us he had heard Chaddy say to the townspeople, "Tell the guerrillas they got the wrong one. I don't know how to raise money. Tell them to trade me for Russell, and he will raise the money." This was his plan to have Russell back in a week. He planned to replace Russell; then of course, he planned to escape.

Marina's brother also told us that according to the townspeople, three of the guerrillas had been girls, one of which was tall and pretty. This brought the first smile to Marina's face. "Maybe Russell can make friends with a 'lady guerrilla,' " she chuckled. "Maybe that is how he will get himself freed."

As we sat around the dinner table, Sharon confided that she thought she would be the one kidnapped. "I thought it all over while I was in the tribe. I realized that God wanted someone to bring the message of repentance and salvation to the guerrillas, and the only way to communicate with them would be to be kidnapped. I felt God was preparing me and strengthening me, so I would be prepared if this should happen. It's strange that I should have been the one to be prepared, and then Russell be kidnapped." Patty and I confessed that we felt much the same way. We had each seriously considered the possibility of being kidnapped when we were up in the mountains with the Kogis.

We wondered if Russell had also been prepared by God emotionally and spiritually for this experience.

The gutless wonder before it was shot up.

CHAPTER 10

Dad, Where Is Your Faith?

I tried to charter a plane to fly out to the ranch, so I could pick up the Cessna 170 and begin a systematic reconnaissance of the area to try and find Russell's location. Finally I found a young woman pilot who had enough courage to fly back into the area. The other pilots had suspended all flights into the region of Canyo Jabon to protest Russell's kidnapping. Our faithful mechanic, Fidel, went with me, bringing a new windshield to be installed in our damaged airplane. When we landed at Chaparral, I looked around for our airplane, but it was not to be seen.

"Chaddy, where have you got the airplane?" I asked.

"I'm sorry, Dad," he replied, "But it's still over at Canyo Jabon."

From his letter we knew that Chaddy had had the plane up in the air, so I assumed it must be at Chaparral. Then Chaddy related the amazing tale of the first and only time he has ever flown an airplane in Colombia.

Even though he didn't have a license and had had only a few hours of instruction in the States in a different kind of aircraft, Chaddy decided that he would fly the Cessna 170 from Canyo Jabon to Chaparral. He wanted to rescue the airplane, and he also wanted to save me from exposure to a possible kidnapping or assassination attempt in Canyo Jabon.

When Chaddy arrived at Canyo Jabon, and the local people found out that he was going to fly the plane out, the whole town turned out to watch the show. Everyone knew that Russell and I were pilots, but no one had ever seen Chaddy sitting in the pilot's seat before. Indeed this was the first time he had sat in that pilot's seat, and it took him a few minutes just to figure out how to get the engine started and what the various levers and instruments were for. His dog, Killer, a huge Rotweiller, would be flying as "co-pilot".

Finally he thought he had everything figured out and gingerly shoved the throttle forward. As he built up speed, he pushed forward on the stick and raised the tail up. By this time his actions were just a little behind the plane's reactions, doing figure S's down the runway. Then he managed to pull the plane up into the air, and he was flying.

And then it happened! The windshield disintegrated all at once with a big bang. The people watching below said pieces of the windshield shot up a hundred feet into the air. Chaddy normally tries to present a calm attitude to everyone and prides himself on acting "cool." However I am sure he was really shaken up when the windshield exploded.

Fortunately Canyo Jabon has a long airstrip and much open grassland, so Chaddy had room to set the airplane down again. After three such bounce-and-go landings, Chaddy finally turned off the switch and the plane landed itself. The Lord must have helped some. He then taxied back with the propeller cutting a swath through the tall grass beyond the strip to where 250 people were standing, amazed at the air show.

By that time Chaddy had recovered his composure and announced, "I never did like airplanes." Killer didn't say anything, but by the disgusted look on his face, it was clear that he didn't like airplanes either.

Back at the ranch, we now still had the major problem of ferrying the plane out of Canyo Jabon. I prevailed on the woman pilot who flew me to Chaparral to fly the mechanic and windshield to Canyo Jabon. She said, "No way am I going to land at a place where three airplanes were shot up and a pilot kidnapped."

"Look, Marlene," I replied, "We're really in a spot. Just land and let the mechanic off, and you can take right off again, before anyone knows you're there."

She got an impish little grin on her face and said, "O.K. I'll do it."

It would take Fidel two days to repair the plane, so I began to make plans with Chaddy as to how we should get the plane out of this dangerous location. Chaddy looked and dressed like a country person and was accepted as such in the area, however it was another matter for me, who obviously looked like a *gringo* and was known to be the owner of the airplane, to show up. I feared that an attack against me might occur. After much thought I unfolded my plan to Chaddy.

As soon as our dugout canoe arrives at the riverbank by Canyo Jabon, I'll make a dash for the airstrip with my shotgun in my hands. You and the others cover me with your guns until I'm in the air, then you high-tail it out of there, back to Chaparral. I'll meet you there. If we're lucky, we'll take them by surprise, and I'll have the plane in the air before anyone can figure out what happened.

Chaddy looked at me with shocked disappointment. "Dad," he said, "Where is your faith? These people need to see how a true Christian reacts under pressure. First of all, you should leave the shotgun home. Then you and I will enter Canyo Jabon as calmly as possible, greeting everyone we meet. We will calmly inspect the location where Russell was kidnapped, then we will go over to the store and drink a Pepsi Cola, talking in a relaxed, friendly manner to all the people. Then we will meander down to the airstrip, inspect the airplane, casually get in and fly away."

I gulped hard, realizing we were going to make tempting targets and stammered, "Yes, Chaddy. . . I guess. . . that's what we should do."

And that's what we did. Well—almost, because half-way through the ordeal, Chaddy whispered to me, "Dad, you're not doing so hot."

"What do you mean?" I whispered back, looking straight ahead.

"You're too tense! Smile!"

So I loosened up, gave them a forced smile, and tried my best to look cool. Most people were friendly, but it was the five or six who wore mean, ugly scowls that had me worried. I was sure they were guerrillas. I wished Chaddy would hurry up and drink his luke-warm Pepsi, but he was taking his time. Finally, after what seemed like an eternity, we got to the plane. What a relief to give it the throttle. Fidel had done a good job, and it flew fine, although there were still bullet holes through the side windows.

As we turned the plane around, Chaddy said, "Give it full throttle and buzz the town." As we went roaring over the main street, I asked, "Chaddy, what was that for?"

He grinned back, "I just wanted to let them know that the Stendal family isn't finished yet."

Now that the airplane was flying again, we started our search. Chaddy made a trip upstream on Canyo Jabon[1], and I flew downstream along the Guaviare River. The task of locating Russell seemed so hopeless. There were countless little streams and areas where they could be holding him. 'If this were a fiction story,' I thought, 'Right at this point we would get a timely breakthrough. We would spot something significant that would lead us to Russell's location, or someone would give us some key information.' However this was not fiction. This was for real, and we got nothing.

There was one more thing I knew I must do. I must try to salvage anything of value that remained at the fish house. It was very hard for me to even consider landing at that strip. I had not been back to that spot since being fired upon by the guerrillas with their automatic weapons. Now I asked the Lord to give me courage to land.

As I lined up on the strip, something close to panic seized me as the trauma of the guerrillas shooting at the plane was replayed through my mind involuntarily. I half expected the guerrillas to open fire again as I touched down. However they weren't there, and I flew back to San Martin with the generator and the compressor.

I began a physical training program, working out with weights and running. 'A little target practice wouldn't hurt either,' I thought. If the opportunity ever came to rescue Russell, I planned to be ready.[2]

---

[1]Caño means a stream or small river. Canyo Jabon is both the name of the town and a river.

[2]At this point we had some further insights as we wrote another letter home. See Appendix B.

CHAPTER 11

Publicity or Secrecy

In Bogota, Ricardo Trillos wanted to do something to help, so he lined up a press conference for Marina with a Christian journalist. He also called the American Embassy, believing they should be informed of the kidnapping. He found the Embassy staff frantic to contact us, so he gave them Gilberto's telephone number, then called us to tell us to send Marina to Bogota as soon as possible.

Patty had barely replaced the receiver after talking with Ricardo, when the phone rang again. It was the Embassy. They were receiving calls from all over the United States asking for information, and by law they could not release it without our written permission. Patty told the woman all we knew and requested that the story be spread far and wide. Patty was so relieved to hear a kindly American voice that she almost wept. The woman promised to see that our families in the States were informed and said she would bring the proper forms to San Martin for our signatures.

Patty told Marina to prepare to go to Bogota for the press conference. Marina seemed agreeable, but after a visit to her family home, she changed her mind. Her father had strictly forbidden her to go to Bogota. He reflected the current Colombian viewpoint of dealing with kidnappings. There was to be *absolutely no publicity*. He thought we should comply with the guerrillas' orders for secrecy. To him, it was clear that we just did not know how to deal with kidnappers. He felt we were risking Russell's life by our willingness to communicate with the media. Nevertheless, our gut-level feeling was for publicity and the public opinion pressure it would put on the guerrillas to release Russell. However, we felt uneasy about opposing Marina and her family's strong opinions. Russell was her husband as well as our son. So the press conference was off; Marina did not go.

At this point we started playing a calculated game. We tried to give enough information to the right people to maintain prayer support at a high level, but also wanted to present an image to the kidnappers' spies, many of whom, we were assured, were constantly watching us, that we were keeping our mouths shut.

In her heart Patty believed all the messages that God had been giving her. It was not simply the case of finding a verse in the Bible and standing on it in faith. She believed these verses had been individually pointed out to her by divine means. However along with the verses was also the knowledge that the final outcome of this kidnapping depended on our walking very close to God and having His wisdom in all the countless decisions that had to be made.

We assured Marina that she and Lisa could have a permanent home with us, no matter what happened. However, we knew that after Russell, her first loyalty was to her family, not to us. If Russell were killed, and the rest of us had to leave the country, she would return to the world she had known before her marriage, and Lisa would fade out of our lives.

Patty's nights were punctuated with prayer for Russell. Towards morning she would sink into a deeper sleep, then awake with a start. For a moment all would seem normal. Then she would remember, 'The kidnappers still have Russell.' The heavy weight would press on her heart again. A tremendous pressure built up behind her eyes. She thought tears would release the pressure, but she couldn't cry. She wanted to talk with a kind, understanding person who spoke English. She eagerly awaited the promised visit from the woman from the American Embassy.

One morning, news appeared in a leftist Colombian paper that Rickey Kirby had been released and had gone to the United States. What joy! This would be a confirmation that all God had revealed to Patty was really true. But Neftali Espitia,

Marina's father was skeptical. He visited Tom, Rickey's ailing husband, in Villavicencio and returned to say that Tom knew nothing of his wife's release. Our spirits sank.

The next day the woman from the U.S. Embassy arrived in a police vehicle driven by two uniformed policemen. We cringed to think of the guerrillas' spies who were surely watching. Families of kidnapped people were not supposed to have anything to do with the police or other authorities according to the unwritten law of the *llanos*.

The Embassy official, accompanied by her Colombian interpreter, had had a hard trip. She felt she had been subjected to cruel and inhuman treatment on the torturous mountain road. Then to top it all off, the hotel in Villavicencio had not had hot water. Her cold shower that morning had ruined her disposition for the day. All we could do was console her. The woman interpreter, however, was kind and friendly. They had visited Tom Kirby and reiterated what Marina's father had told us. No one knew anything about Mrs. Kirby's alleged release—not Tom, not her children in the United States, and certainly not the U.S. Embassy.

"Her U.S. passport has elapsed," the official told us. "There is no way she could have left Colombia without going through my office."

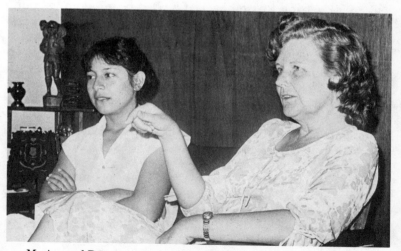

Marina and Patty contemplate the effects of Russell's kidnapping.

Tom believed that his wife had died in captivity. (She suffered from a heart condition.) He thought this news release had been a cover-up so that the rank and file of people in the *llanos* would not hold the guerrillas responsible for her death. The Embassy concurred in this opinion as being the most logical.

We signed the necessary papers for the Embassy and prepared a news release to be given out as requested in both English and Spanish. The Embassy group then visited the local police station.

The next day a number of people came to our house to tell us excitedly, "Yes! It is true that Mrs. Kirby has been released! She was seen in San Martin yesterday!" Up went our hopes again; then down to rock bottom. It was the Embassy official who had been seen at the police station. To the people of San Martin, all middle-aged, North American women looked just about the same.

Every day it seemed, several of Russell's friends came by to express their indignation and sympathy about the kidnapping. One day we had a visit from a close friend of Russell's who was an officer in the secret police in Bogota. I was surprised by the depths of his fury and rage towards the kidnappers. To his way of thinking, no torture would be too harsh for the captors if they were caught. To my surprise he stated that we had a better chance of getting Russell back if he had been taken by an established guerrilla group rather than common criminals seeking a ransom.

A reporter was sent out to see us by Associated Press. He was very understanding. "I wouldn't want to put anyone's life at risk just to get a story," he told us. Later a discreet article appeared in the U.S. press. But the journalist had raised a new problem. "I have covered kidnappings all over the world," he commented, "And this doesn't fit the pattern. I don't think the guerrillas have him." Fear gripped our hearts. Was he then being held by "common criminals?"

On Sunday Patty, Gloria and Uriel conducted Sunday School in the underprivileged neighborhood. Afterwards they visited many families and shared with them the story of the kidnapping and the verses of hope that God had given Patty. The people all promised to pray for Russell.

One day another visitor showed up. It was Fernando Suarez,

who had formerly sold fish to Russell from his fish trap at the beautiful Tomachipan Falls out in the jungle. He came to express his sympathy as had many others. When we told him that we thought the ELN or the EPL had Russell, he said, "No way. The FARC[1] is the dominant guerrilla group in the *llanos*. They wouldn't let a rival group come in and kidnap a person in their territory." We had had a short-lived hope of enlisting the powerful FARC to help us get Russell back from the smaller guerrilla group, but now it appeared the FARC itself had him and had tried to shift the blame to another group to avoid adverse public opinion.

After hearing our story, Fernando looked thoughtful. Finally he said, "I think I'm just the person to help you out. I know you folks well, having done business with Russell for years. I also have dealings with the muchachos ("boys" as the guerrillas are locally called). I can set up a meeting for you with some of them. But I will have to have your word that you won't cause them a problem by identifying them to the police." We told him to go ahead. It was our first hope of penetrating the wall of silence surrounding our son's disappearance.

By this time, a telephone had been installed in our home in San Martin. We had submitted our request for the first time in 1975, but since the telephone company wanted us to pay for five blocks of telephone poles and wire in addition to the regular charges, we had no phone. After Russell was captured, the phone company decided that the telephone wire could be strung on the electric poles and expedited the installation of our phone within a week. They were confident the kidnappers would contact us by telephone.

Several days after Fernando's visit, we received a call from his wife. They had set up a meeting at their home in Villavicencio, and they wanted Patty, Marina, and me to appear the next evening at seven o'clock. I was in Bogota and Patty vainly tried to contact me. As the hour of the meeting drew near, Marina and Patty prepared to go. The pressure had continued to build up in Patty's head, and now she had a constant pain and pressure behind her eyes. She realized that since I was not

---

[1]*Fuerzas Armadas Revolucionarios de Colombia* (Revolutionary Armed Forces of Colombia)—This is the largest guerrilla group in Colombia. It operates mostly in the rural areas and is backed by International Communism.

going to be there, she would have to make the decisions and deal with the guerrillas. She had no idea what would happen. She knew that Marina expected that we would just get them to come down to a more reasonable demand, and then we would pay it. Patty felt that she should prepare Marina for the eventuality that we would feel hesitant to pay a ransom at all.

Patty and I were well aware that many missions had gone on record as refusing to pay ransom. We were members of a small mission and had never received any guidelines regarding ransom. We had always felt that as we walked in the Spirit, we would be guided on such issues when and if the time came.

As Patty faced the possibility that she and Marina would be negotiating with the guerrillas in a few hours, she felt the urgency to communicate to Marina the fact that many people would feel a moral reluctance about ransom. Patty called Marina to the patio and as gently as possible started to explain that some people felt it was wrong to pay money to subversives. She thought she was being very diplomatic and as tactful as possible, but Marina's reaction was worse than Patty had expected. For the first time, Marina exploded. She burst into tears, saying that we were terrible people who cared more for money than the life of our son, and that she would see to it that his life was not lost because of our unrealistic ideas.

It would soon be time to leave for Villavo. Patty started thinking how it would be to sit in Fernando's living room face to face with one of Russell's kidnappers. She remembered what Gilberto had said about their violence, and she was overwhelmed by a feeling of rage against the guerrillas. Patty, like Marina, is usually a calm, self-controlled person, and this reaction of rage both amazed and frightened her. White-faced and trembling, she dropped into a chair on the patio. Sharon offered to go with Marina, and Patty retired to her bedroom, spending the rest of the afternoon in prayer.

Neither the guerrillas nor Fernando kept the appointment. It seemed like our one chance of finding out what had happened to Russell had come to nothing.

CHAPTER 12

Words I Would Regret

September 3, 1983

I left for Chaparral to confer with Chaddy and continue the aerial search for Russell. Patty and Sharon accompanied me part way. Patty was still experiencing the severe pain in her head and pressure behind her eyes. They would spend a few days at Lomalinda, the Wycliffe Bible Translators' Center, and maybe the trip would be beneficial.

The Colombian Branch of the Wycliffe Bible Translators had gone through a kidnapping experience in 1981 that ended in the death of the victim, Chet Bitterman[1], and the hurt was still fresh. Sharon and Patty were greeted at the airplane by Will Kindberg, a former branch director. Will was extremely gracious and sensitive to Patty's needs. He wanted the visit to be beneficial and did not want her to have to tell the story of the kidnapping over and over. It was decided that Patty and Sharon would spend the time in the homes of their closest friends, and a time was arranged for Patty to speak in the Lomalinda auditorium to all who wished to hear the story.

The visit to Lomalinda helped Patty greatly. She was able to express her feelings to sympathetic listeners, who would support us in prayer until the ordeal was over, no matter how long it took.

On Sunday afternoon the three of us returned home. Gloria

---

[1] *Called to Die*, by Steve Estes, Wycliffe Bible Translators, Huntington Beach, CA 92647.

ran down the road to meet us as we neared the house. She had two groups of visitors that she was trying to keep separated. Fernando Suarez had returned, and he and Neftali Espitia, Russell's father-in-law, were in a bedroom waiting to talk to me about a contact with the guerrillas, and Jaime Gonzales, a radio expert and close friend of Russell's was on the patio also waiting to talk with me. He had brought two expensive radios that he offered to loan us to replace the ailing, old, two-way radios Russell had bought years before for the fish business. He wanted to help us maintain reliable radio contact with Chaddy at Chaparral.

Fernando was a typical Colombian small-time businessman without strong political opinions, who was willing to rub shoulders with the guerrillas, drug traffickers or whatever, in order to keep afloat economically. Jaime Gonzales represented another group of Colombians with more knowledge of world-wide political issues and with strong political convictions, who although deploring much in the present Colombian government, was strongly committed to democracy and stood solidly against Communism. Each one was motivated by compassion for us and Russell in our grim situation and had come to offer aid in his own way. Gloria instinctively knew that it would be best to keep them apart.

I went into the bedroom to talk with Fernando and Neftali while Patty sat on the patio with the Gonzales family. Fernando had found some people who would go into the guerrilla-held territory to find out if the FARC had Russell, but we would have to pay the expense of chartering an airplane and supplying them with several weeks provisions. I offered to save money by flying them myself but was informed that only certain planes and pilots were allowed into guerrilla territory.

We decided to accept Fernando's offer, as it was the only opportunity we had to contact Russell's kidnappers. We also thankfully accepted the use of the radios, and the next day I dropped one off at Chaparral, and after another futile air search, returned to San Martin. We now had regular radio contact with Chaddy at Chaparral. Jaime continued to visit us regularly to make sure the radios were working. He drank gallons of strong coffee and became a trusted friend and confidant as the kidnapping dragged on.

My next job was to go to Bogota and scrape up money to give to Fernando for chartering the plane. It was not easy, but in three days I had it together and handed it over to him. We also entrusted him with two letters, malaria medicine, and a Spanish Bible with the hope that these items would reach Russell.

"Try to get them to reduce their demand in half," I instructed Fernando. "Then we can start negotiating from a more reasonable figure." Little did I know how much I would regret those words.

CHAPTER 13

The Older and the Younger

Week after week had gone by since Russell was kidnapped. We were unable to ascertain his condition or location, and we heard nothing from the kidnappers. We began to believe they had killed him, since we hadn't received any ransom demand. I would wake up in the morning, and for a few seconds I would feel normal, and then it would hit me. *The guerrillas have taken our son Russell.* A cold terror would grip me by the throat.

Every father has dreams of his son fulfilling great promise and accomplishing things of which he can be proud. I had had very high hopes for Russell, and being my first son, I spent a lot of time training him in every useful activity I could. He was very intelligent and possessed many natural abilities. At sixteen months there was nothing he couldn't repeat after us, and at eighteen months he was totally fluent. He played with boys much older than he, and they were sure that he was their age and was some kind of midget.

When Russell was small, Patty and I were very active in youth work. We were the sponsors of the youth group in our local church, and I was the captain of the Boys' Brigade, which was similar to the Boy Scouts. Patty was very active in the Pioneer Girls, a similar girls' organization and was chairman of their camp committee. Russell accompanied us to many of these meetings and was like a little mascot at the girls' summer camp. He had a great many Christian young people as role models.

One of the mothers who had a son in the Boys' Brigade came

to me one day. "Chad," she said, "My boy is fifteen years old now, and I think it is time for him to make a decision for Christ. Will you please take care of it, as I can't do a thing with him."

Since this is one of the regular goals of the Boys' Brigade, I told her we were already doing everything we could. I thought to myself, 'She and her husband should have been training the boy through his entire childhood.' Now the task of leading him to the Lord was greatly complicated because he was completely out of control and totally rebellious. He caused disruptions in the meetings that hindered the work with the other boys.

We had an idea at that time that there was an age of accountability. We thought that when a boy reached twelve to fifteen years of age, he would become morally accountable, and this would be the ideal time to press him to commit his life to the Lord. My ideas on this were soon to change, as Russell was gaining spiritual understanding rapidly. We went through many Bible stories, and Russell was always very interested. Finally I realized that he was close to being able to receive Jesus as his own personal Lord and Savior, and I said to Patty as I went to work, "Soon Russell is going to ask where God is or where He lives. I don't want you to just tell him God lives in heaven, but to let him know that God also lives in our hearts."

That very same day Russell, who was almost two years old, climbed up into his mother's lap and asked, "Where does God live?"

"God lives in heaven, but He also lives in people's hearts," was her reply.

"Does He live in your heart?" he wanted to know.

"Yes," Patty answered, "He lives in my heart."

Does He live in Daddy's heart?" was his next question. Patty said, "Yes", and then Russell asked about Stuart and Eleanor, our best friends, and their two boys, Dennis and Terry. Patty said that yes, God lived in Stuart and Eleanor and Dennis' hearts, but she wasn't sure about Terry because he was very young and probably hadn't asked God to live in his heart yet.

At that Russell got very concerned and asked if God lived in his heart. Patty told him that she didn't think he had asked Him yet either. Russell got right down off his mother's lap and knelt beside the bed. "Come into my heart, God! Come into my heart, Jesus!" he called out in a very loud voice. Then he jumped up and putting his hand over his heart, he exclaimed, "He's in there!"

As a youngster, Russell had his share of temper tantrums and willful disobedience, but after this conversion experience, we observed a significant change in his attitude. He had consciously put his will on the Lord's side, and we could reason with him, pray with him, and get his cooperation when he had done something wrong. More important, I believe the Lord Himself began training and teaching him.

I believe a father's relationship with his son must change a little every day, giving the boy a little more responsibility and substituting a living relationship with God for blind obedience to his father, until when the boy is about eighteen, he is totally under God's control, and father and son are in many ways equal adults. Of course some things, such as respect and honor for the father, never change, yet the son must eventually have his own personal relation with God and be responsible to Him alone for his actions. The final authority for the boy's actions passes from the earthly father to the heavenly Father.

Our second son, Chaddy, was eighteen months younger than Russell. Chaddy had a difficult time growing up as the second son. He was at an unfair disadvantage in competing with his brother. One time when our youth group put on a program at

Chaddy and Russell help their father build a jungle hut.

a nursing home, Russell and Chaddy came along. Russell sang a song and quoted a Bible verse from memory. When Russell got done, Chaddy, who was too young to do any of those things but didn't want to be left out, stepped forward in front of the group and exclaimed in a loud voice, "Me too!"

Little by little, a problem developed between Russell and Chaddy, and it was difficult for me to obtain the right balance in my relationship with them. Chaddy had an entirely different personality from Russell. He had special qualities, just as valuable as Russell's, but completely different. It was hard for me to maintain the same intense training and relationship with the second son as with the first, since Russell was older and could do more things with me. Also, Russell's spiritual insight was increasing every day.

Finally, one day when I was working as the project engineer of the Farmington NIKE missile base, I decided to explain missions to Russell for his bedtime story. He sat on my knee while I showed him actual pictures of life among an Indian tribe of Ecuador. These pictures showed life as it really was among these descendants of the Incas. These Indians lived in abject poverty and misery. One series of pictures showed them going to market and then getting drunk. After this there was fighting and finally a picture on the following morning of an Indian woman waiting for her husband to sober up, so they could return up the trail to their home for another week of the same.

Russell had never seen or heard of anyone living in such poverty and sin before in his young life, and so he asked, "Why do they live like that?"

"I don't know, Russ," I replied, "I guess they just don't know how to live any differently."

"Why don't they know how to live any better?" Russell persisted.

"I guess it's because no one has helped them or shown them any better," I answered.

Russell was indignant. "Why hasn't anyone helped them?"

To this I didn't have an answer, and so I said, "Well, Russ, I guess nobody much cares about these people, and that is why nobody has gone to help them."

"You care about them, don't you Dad?"

Hesitantly I answered, "Yes, Son, I care."

His next question really brought me up short. "Then why don't we go and help them?"

The logic of his question still to this day seems reasonable. If there were people living in such desperate conditions, and no one else would help them, why didn't we go and help them? I couldn't answer this question. At five years old, the boy had me on the spot. I didn't want to lose the confidence of my son, so I finally said, "You can't just go off to South America and work with Indians. That would be missionary work. Why, God would have to call you to be a missionary. He would have to go before you and provide for all your needs. He would have to open all the doors." I went on and on, and put the whole responsibility on God. It was all His problem.

Just when it seemed that I had been able to slip out from under the responsibility that the question raised, I noticed that Russell wasn't listening to me anymore. He had gotten off my lap and was kneeling by the side of the couch, praying aloud as he did every night. "Dear Lord, please call my parents to be missionaries," he prayed. Had we not been telling him that God answers prayer?

Well, God does answer prayer, and God gave to both me and Patty a very definite call to Colombia, South America. He did go before us and provided for all our needs, even as He promised. When we drew close to the Lord and turned everything over to Him, we were able to hear His voice, and He directed us, straight as an arrow, to the Kogi tribe in the high mountains of northern Colombia.

When we were making plans to attend the University of North Dakota to study linguistics, Patty asked the Lord to supply our registration fees from an unusual source as a sign that all our financial needs would be provided. I was somewhat frustrated by this request, as I had to apply for a leave of absence from my job, and we could do nothing until we were accepted at the University. The needed funds were $15. apiece.

One morning in balancing the family checkbook, Patty found an error in our favor of $15. "That certainly is an unexpected source," I declared, since all previous checkbook errors had lowered our balance, and got my application ready to mail.

Russell and I got into the car. I would leave him off at the Christian school on my way to work. We stopped at the mailbox.

Chad leads the family in devotions about the time that Russell prayed that his family would be missionaries.

"Why aren't we sending in Mother's application too?" he asked. As usual, he didn't miss a thing.

"We have to wait for another $15. in order to send hers in," I replied.

Russell pulled himself up to his full height and got a deep tone in his voice which he used when he had to say something important. "I want you to go right down to the bank and take $15. out of my savings account. I have decided to send Mother to the Institute of Linguistics this summer."

The next day we visited the bank and drew out Russell's money. He solemnly handed Patty $15. and returned the rest to his account. From that time on, he felt like Patty's sponsor in our missionary endeavor. At the university he helped with the younger children, so that we could study, and he prayed for her before each examination. When grades came out, he demanded to see them. He had just finished first grade at a private, Christian school. His first report card had been mostly B's with a few C's, and his teacher told us he was capable of better work. "I'm spending money to send you to this school," I told him. "I'll give you a treat for each A that you get, and a spanking for each C." His final report card was all A's.

Now he demanded good grades from his mother. "I'm spending my money to send you here," he told her. Luckily she got all A's and B's.

After our linguistic study, I returned to my job as office engineer for a large lock and dam project in downtown Minneapolis. In a few weeks I would be resigning from the U.S. Army Corps of Engineers permanently. Just then a job opportunity notice came to my attention. An engineer was needed to take charge of all construction on the island of Guam. I had all the qualifications for the position. It was a tailor-made temptation. I had spent time on Guam in the '40's, and I loved the place—beautiful white sandy beaches, no mosquitoes, and no malaria. There was even an indigenous tribe on the island. I could practice my newly acquired linguistic skills in my spare time. I'll send at least a tithe of my income to the Colombian branch of the Wycliffe Bible Translators, I rationalized, and we will save enough money to be self-supporting missionaries later.

At the supper table I was telling the family about this job opportunity, stressing the therapeutic effect of the climate of Guam on our health. At last Russell could stand it no longer. He spoke up in the firmest, deepest voice he could muster. "I thought God called us to be missionaries in Colombia."

"He did, Son," I replied, "We are still going to do that, but first we are going to this beautiful place etc., etc."

Once again Russell's firm voice interrupted, "Do we have to take the easy way?"

The child's words pierced me to the heart. I finally, after much prayer and consideration, decided to resign from my government job and go to the Jungle Training Center of the Wycliffe Bible Translators in southern Mexico. After that came three more months of linguistic study, and we were on our way to Colombia. Both boys emptied their savings accounts to help buy our tickets to Colombia.

That this was the Lord's will was later confirmed. A few months later, a typhoon hit the island of Guam, causing widespread destruction. All dependents were sent home, no missionary work would have been possible, and our funds would have been wasted in maintaining two households.

Russell continued to be very helpful in Colombia, and when I was asked to begin the construction of the translation center at Lomalinda, he was right by my side, living in a jungle hammock, being helpful by carrying water and washing the dishes. I was Russell's school teacher during much of his schooling. He completed high school by correspondence. I helped him set up all the laboratory experiments for physics and chemistry. Later, when he took the college entrance exams, he was in the upper one percent in science.

Russell accompanied me on many trips to isolated Kogi villages and on other surveys into new territories to establish contact with new tribes. He followed in my footsteps, learning to fly, and became a fine jungle pilot. He was also growing in spiritual maturity, and it seemed that all my hopes and prayers would be fulfilled in his life.

All these memories and expectations for Russell's future were now shattered with the brutal fact:

The guerrillas have taken our son!

CHAPTER 14

Communication from the Guerrillas

On Tuesday, September 6, Chaddy called on the radio to say that he was taking a boat and motor to check out the area downstream on the Guaviare River. This area was much more noted for guerrilla activity than was the area upstream. He expected to be back the next day for our regular contact time. The following Saturday I returned from Bogota and found Patty and Gloria extremely worried because Chaddy had missed four days of radio contact.

It was now four weeks since Russell had been kidnapped and there had been no communication from his captors. I was becoming convinced that they had killed him, and that was why we heard nothing. Now Chaddy was missing, and the most probable conclusion was that we had now lost both of our sons. That Saturday night was the most difficult night I have ever experienced. Early the next morning I readied the plane to search for Chaddy, a very dangerous assignment in itself.

Such pessimistic thoughts may seem like a lack of faith, but the fact remains that the Lord allowed the death of John the Baptist and James, the brother of John, while Peter and John were miraculously released from prison. God has the right to decide who will become a martyr and who will be miraculously delivered. We have to be ready to accept either alternative from the Lord's hand.[1]

---

[1]The Apostle Paul stated this concept . . . but with full courage now as always Christ will be honored in my body, whether by life or by death. (Philippians 1:20)

Gloria slept with the radio turned on in case Chaddy should call, and early Sunday while I prepared to leave, she was at the microphone trying to make contact with Chaparral. It was painful to see the anguish on Gloria's face as she kept calling, and no one answered.

Guillermo Romero, Russell's good friend and long-time employee joined me for the flight. We didn't know if or when we would be returning. Just as we were loading up for the flight to the ranch, Patty came running out. Chaddy had answered the radio! His trip downriver had taken much longer than expected. Chaddy said that everything was fine at Chaparral, but he had no news of Russell.

That afternoon we received thrilling news—Russell was alive!

Several members of the Espitia family came to our house with some Polaroid photos of Russell in captivity and a letter in Russell's handwriting, but obviously not composed by him. The letter was dated ten days after the kidnapping, and had taken eighteen days to arrive. Marina's sister, Rosario, had brought the letter from Mapiripan that morning.

Her story was the following: An elderly man had been given two letters by the FARC and was told to give them only to Raul Espitia, Marina's oldest brother, in Mapiripan. Raul happened to be spending the week in San Martin, so the man couldn't find him and kept the letters in his possession. Finally, the man passed the letters to Rosario and her brother, Hernan, who were the only ones present in the Espitias' house in Mapiripan. The letter to Raul contained detailed instructions for contacting the guerrillas, but by this time the date had already passed.

Rosario and Hernan followed the directions in a vain attempt to meet with the guerrillas, but it was too late. Rosario decided to bring us the other letter, which was addressed to me, and crossed paths with Raul who was on his way back to Mapiripan.

Although Russell looked forlorn and dejected in the photos, we were overjoyed to know that he was still alive. We studied the pictures in detail, hoping for some clue as to his whereabouts. He was sitting on a fallen log in a clearing in the jungle. The background consisted entirely of leaves and branches. The site could have been most anywhere, although Chaddy could tell by the vegetation that Russell was on high ground in an area never flooded by the river. That meant he was well removed from the river's edge and explained why no one had seen him or his captors. On the log beside him was an enameled cup and a small loaf of bread, common items in all of Colombia. There were no pertinent clues; all we knew was that he was alive and in the jungle.

The letter sounded very strange, but it definitely was Russell's handwriting.

August 24, 1983

Señor Chad Stendal
Dear Father,

Receive my greeting. I hope this finds everyone all right. I find myself in a situation which I have never wanted to happen. It's hard; it's difficult and critical.

Only the morale which I acquired in my home and later in my life makes it possible for me to remain firm in my intentions.

I have been kidnapped. I lament this situation. Without your help it can never be resolved. I am in as much need of parental help as I was as an infant. Put yourselves in touch with Raul Espitia. He has received the instructions of my captors.

It is necessary to be supremely careful. Don't let the authorities know of the development of the negotiation of my release.

As is natural, I am very anxious to return to freedom. It depends on you how long I will have to endure this inhuman situation. I trust your capability and your intelligence, just as I have many memories of your love. I send this to you with an affectionate *abrazo* (hug).

Cordially,
Russell

This was not at all the way Russell would compose a letter. We correctly assumed that the letter had been written by his captors, and he had been forced to copy it in his handwriting. I immediately went to Villavo in an attempt to cancel the arrangement with Fernando Suarez, but it was too late. His friends had already left for the jungle to make contact with the FARC.

We were wondering how to proceed and were hoping the kidnappers would contact us again. We hadn't long to wait. Two days later another letter was delivered to us by the Espitia family.

September, 1983

Señor Chadwick M. Stendal
Dear Dad,

I hope that this finds everything all right at home. I am all right, but I want very much to get out of here.

I am informing you that my captors have chosen my brother-in-law, Raul Espitia, as the mediator to negotiate my freedom. I have complete confidence in Raul and hope that you have the same.

I also want to tell you that my captors are professionals, and in my opinion, it would be completely useless for you to try to rescue me by means of the authorities. You must keep completely silent about the negotiations which you will make by means of Raul. I tell you that any lack of confidence that you have in Raul will make me have to stay here much longer.

Your son,
Russell Stendal

There was also a letter to Marina from Russell and one to Raul from the kidnappers asking 40 million pesos ($500,000) and giving instructions for a contact. Now we had to decide whether to negotiate.

We met in the Espitias' kitchen. My inclination was to refuse to negotiate, but Marina was irate at my hesitancy. We had no money to offer, which was difficult even for the Espitias to understand, as most Colombians think that all North Americans are wealthy. Patty was not at all sure about paying ransom but thought we should enter into a negotiation. "The Lord has told me that Russell is there to be a witness. If we don't negotiate, they may kill him right away, and his witness will be ended. If we offer some low amount and keep the negotiation alive, it will give Russell more time to witness to his captors and something else might happen," she reasoned.

Marina's father pointed out that not only was Russell's life at risk, but the lives of his two sons, Raul and Hernan, as well. They had entered into the dealings with the guerrillas, and if we refused to negotiate, the guerrillas might retaliate by killing them. They were very vulnerable, living as they did in Mapiripan.

I was not sure the guerrillas would release Russell to us, even if we paid a ransom.

Chaddy had already verbally offered the guerrillas 500,000 pesos ($6,250), which was what he figured he could raise by selling all his assets. Patty thought we should reiterate that offer in the note that I was sending to the guerrillas by means of the Espitia brothers.

It was an afternoon charged with emotion. I finally authorized the Espitias to verbally offer 500,000 pesos, but I refused to put it in writing. They were not pleased, but the tension relaxed, and they departed to try their luck with the guerrillas.

I began to pray about this matter and to study the Bible to see what God had to say about ransom.

Photo taken by Russell's kidnappers on August 24, 10 days after his kidnapping.   Photo by F.A.R.C.

CHAPTER 15

The Negotiation

Our friends and acquaintances in San Martin were very concerned about Russell and sympathetic with us in our suffering. Every time we went out on the street, we were asked if we had heard from the kidnappers. Up until this time we could honestly say no, we hadn't. Now we were cautioned that even though a contact had been made, we must continue to say that we knew nothing. Patty didn't feel that she could go out and face the questions. She didn't want to tell lies to her friends, and neither did she want to jeopardize the contact with the kidnappers. She stayed at home and stopped visiting people.

The Espitia brothers returned. The contact had not gone well. The guerrillas wanted only to know how much money we would give them in exchange for Russell. When they realized that the money was not readily forthcoming. their mood turned ugly. The brothers had not even mentioned the 500,000 pesos we had authorized them to offer. They felt the guerrillas would hit them for daring to offer such a ridiculously low sum. The next contact would be on Sunday. We were told to prepare a letter with a concrete offer.

We wrote a letter[1] to send to the guerrillas, agonizing and praying over each paragraph. We wanted the guerrillas to understand who we really were. We wanted to share our faith with them; however we did not want to needlessly antagonize them and goad them into killing Russell.

---

[1]These letters were all written in Spanish. In the translation we have tried to retain the Spanish "flavor."

Casa Agape
San Martin, Meta
September 17, 1983

Señores Captores of Russell Stendal
Esteemed neighbors,

In January we will complete twenty years in Colombia. We have lived in peace with all our neighbors. So then, why is it, if you have an argument with us, that you didn't come to our house to discuss it over a cup of *tinto*? Or if not that, why didn't you at least send us a letter of warning? It was not necessary for you to risk a dangerous kidnapping. Nevertheless, we are not harboring a grudge, since we are Christians, and the Lord teaches us that we have to pardon those that do us harm as a condition for our own pardon.

I believe that this entire incident is an error. If you are asking half a million dollars of ransom, then you have confused us with rich people, which we are not. It seems that you think you have caught a whale, when actually you have only caught a little sunfish.

Or maybe you have believed that all North Americans have a lot of money. You don't know that at this moment there are ten millions of North Americans without employment, and the majority of the people are workers, as was my father. Actually we are not Yankees; we have our roots in the country of Norway. My mother was born in Norway and worked there to earn passage money to the United States. She came alone and married my father, who was also a descendent of Norwegians. They only had a grade school education, and I am the only child. I don't have any other family than my father and mother, who now are more than 80 years old and live by means of a small pension for retired workers on the railroad.

They didn't have money to send me to the University, but I managed to pay my own way for five years of study, and I graduated as a civil engineer in the year 1956, taking eight years to do so, (taking time out to work). I worked as a civil engineer for a number of years, until God convinced me that it was more important to work with and help needy people than to work with concrete and steel as an engineer. So I entered the university again and changed my profession to be a linguist and an anthropologist. I have a master's degree from the University of North Dakota, and I came to

Colombia as a missionary to the Indians.

I lived with my family in a tiny mud hut built by the Indians for more than thirteen years, preparing reading materials and treating medically more than ten people a day. Russell was eight years old and has lived much of his life with Indians in a house with a mud floor and a grass roof.

On August 14th, Russell was attending a meeting in Canyo Jabon with the purpose of transporting the cold storage equipment from the fish house to Canyo Jabon and sell it on credit, so that the people there could form a cooperative. A band of strangers took the town by surprise, and Russell surrendered to avoid violence.

We have many friends in the region. Hundreds of people have expressed indignation and sorrow at the incident. The Stendal family is very united, and we have everything in common. Why don't we cooperate in helping the poorest country people? My wife and I would be glad to visit you. We have a projector and portable generator and can show pictures of the life of Jesus. These are 12 movies of 30 minutes each in color. We also have Bibles to distribute. It would be a pleasure for us to give each member of your group a Bible or New Testament gratis.

Because we walk with God, we are not afraid of anyone. As Jesus told us in St. Luke chapter 12, verses 4 and 5: "I tell you my friends, don't fear those who can only kill the body and after that can do nothing. I will tell you who you should fear. Fear Him (God) who after death can cast you in hell. Yes, I tell you, fear Him!"

To be a true Christian, it is not enough to just believe that Jesus died and rose again. We have to also identify in the death of Jesus, so that the power that raised Him from the dead can function in us. That is to say that we have to die to all the desires of the flesh (sin), so that the Spirit of God can live in us, giving us the power to live lives agreeable to Him.

It is not possible to correct social injustice by changing the government. You have to change the people first. This only God can do. God has promised to change men's hearts on two conditions: (1) Repent of all the bad that you have done, (2) Put faith in Jesus to help you to change your life until you are doing those things that please God, not by outside rules, but by an interior change—a new heart.[2]

Once you know the truth, I am sure that you will act responsibly and release Russell.

Attentively,
Chadwick M. Stendal

We asked several Colombians to read the letter to correct any mistakes in Spanish. They were aghast at the content. They thought we should have a subservient, ingratiating attitude. But we thought this was a great opportunity to present the guerrillas with the Gospel. We knew they would read every word carefully to see what we were offering them in exchange for Russell.

We sent a box for Russell, including books in English and Spanish, a Spanish Bible, a T-shirt, boots, and socks. Sharon hid some "sweet tarts" that she had brought from the U.S. in the toe of one of the boots, thinking they would give him the boots, but that we would have to sneak the candy to him. We later learned that he only received two of the Spanish books, the T-shirt, and the "sweet tarts." He used the candy to play a trick on his guards.[3] They did not give him the Bible.

Chad flew the letter and box to Chaddy at Chaparral. Chaddy took it upriver by dugout canoe to Raul in Mapiripan. Raul took it farther upriver to the rendezvous with the guerrillas. In San Martin we anxiously awaited the outcome.

Late that night Chaddy called us on the radio. This contact had gone better. The guerrillas had come down to 20 million pesos ($250,000). Of course this demand was still astronomical, but the fact that they had cut it in half was most encouraging.

Then Chaddy gave us startling news. The same guerrillas

---

[2] Some people do not believe that repentance is necessary for salvation. The Bible teaches otherwise, and God commands "all men everywhere to <u>repent</u>," (Acts 17:30). Repentance implies a sorrow for sin and a desire to allow God to change your life to conform to the image of Jesus Christ, (Romans 8:29). The verses stating that repentance is necessary are very numerous. The Lord Jesus Christ himself says, "unless you <u>repent</u>, you shall all . . . perish" (Luke 13:3). Peter states on the day of Pentecost, "<u>Repent</u> and be baptized, and you shall receive the Holy Spirit," (Acts 2:38). There are dozens of similar verses.

[3] After giving his guards a sample of the candy, Russell told them it was poison and that they would all drop dead in five minutes. The story is told in *Rescue the Captors*.

Upper Kogi village of Mamarongo.

Kogi village, airstrip, and our A-frame.

Sharon with Kogis during the epidemic.

Patty's smiling face cheers up the otherwise sober Kogis.

The Cessna 170, the old gutless wonder has never failed us.

We have a species of catfish that weigh up to 400 lbs. and are very good eating.

The frontier village of Mapiripan on the Guaviare River.

Russell at Chaparral with the famous *llanero* (cowboy) *Mano de Tigre.*

who had Russell also had Rickey Kirby. They wanted to use this same line of communication to negotiate with Tom Kirby. They said they had broken off communications with the Kirby family because the American Embassy had been advised. They warned us: WE WERE TO TALK TO NO ONE! Only Tom Kirby, the Espitias, and ourselves were to know that they were negotiating Rickey's release. The captors demanded utmost secrecy.

CHAPTER 16

Tom Kirby

The next day Patty and I drove to Villavicencio to take the news to Tom Kirby. He was out of the hospital and was living with a Baptist missionary family who had graciously taken him into their home and were caring for him. Tom was extremely crippled with arthritis and could barely walk with the aid of crutches. His physical condition was bad, and he was very depressed. We were aghast at his condition.

Gently we told him our story. Several minutes passed before he grasped the fact that Rickey was still alive. We had the feeling that he was so convinced of her death, that he was just hanging on to life in order to hear the worst confirmed. The news we brought was not what he was expecting.

Slowly he began to adjust to the new development and perked up a bit as we continued the conversation. Rickey had now been in captivity five months. He could see little hope of getting her out alive. He said that financially, he had lost everything and could not begin a negotiation.

Thursday, September 22, we had our third contact with the guerrillas. I sent a letter and copies of documents to establish the low state of our finances. The next day, Hernan Espitia arrived with a letter addressed to Tom Kirby. It was to be delivered into Tom Kirby's hands by Hernan personally with utmost secrecy. We jumped into the Toyota and sped off for Villavo—Patty, Marina, Hernan, and myself.

The day before, we had received a phone call from the woman at the Embassy. By now we were paranoid about any activity that would cause the guerrillas to break off the contact. She wanted to come out to see us again, but I asked her not to do so. She was quite uncooperative and said that the only way she could be stopped from coming was by having the request in writing. Since she planned to leave Bogota early the next morning, there was no way to get a written request to her in time. As forcefully as possible, I asked her to stay away, and said I would come to her office in Bogota with the signed request as soon as possible. Patty immediately typed up a formal request for both Tom and me to sign.

We found Tom a bit less depressed than on the previous visit. His letter from the guerrillas contained Polaroid photos and a letter from Rickey. Looking at the pictures, Tom broke down and cried. "Look at her! After all she has been through, she can still smile!" he exclaimed through his tears.

The letter was written in her own words. She reminisced about the past and sounded rather sad, but composed. She sent greetings to each family member but gave no real information as to her physical condition nor instructions for her family.

We were sitting on the sofa conversing with Tom when a huge, green and white van of the secret police pulled up in front of the house. The woman from the Embassy and her interpreter alighted. This was the last thing I wanted to have happen. The guerrillas consider the American Embassy and the CIA to be the same thing. "I told you not to come here!" I roared at the woman.

"I did not come to see you!" she bellowed at me. "I came to see Tom Kirby!"

At that moment I presented her with the typed request that Tom had just finished signing. She had no choice but to climb back in the van and return to Bogota over the winding mountain road. We could only hope that some informant of the guerrillas had not seen her entering the house.

Tom still felt that he had no resources left with which to make an offer. The missionary who had befriended Tom came home at that point. He was handling all Tom's affairs, and he convinced Tom that an offer, albeit a low one, could be made. Tom agreed, and the missionary promised to bring the letter to us in San Martin in time for the contact with the guerrillas the next day.

Patty had brought her Bible along. She had been feeling that she should share her verses of hope with Tom. He still had little expectation of Rickey's release. We knew that he had never had much use for religion, so it was with a little trepidation that she started. He listened politely as Pat related how God had spoken to her on the day of Russell's kidnapping, assuring her that it would lead to Rickey's release. She shared the verses from Isaiah which had been so comforting to her. Tom didn't say much, but we felt that a little more of the despair had melted out of his heart.

CHAPTER 17

A Secret Message in Code

We hurried home to prepare for the contact the next day. Tom gave Patty medicine and a blood pressure cuff for Rickey. Patty packed it along with some books in English. I wrote a letter offering to pay a million pesos for Russell's release, having made a thorough study of the subject in the Scriptures and finding no commandment against paying a ransom. To the contrary, salvation was referred to as a ransom given to redeem us. I also discovered that the early Church regularly raised money to redeem Christian slaves. Patty was equally convinced that we should offer the million pesos. "I'm sure Russell's life, if he is released, will do more good for the Kingdom of God than the million pesos will do for the Communists' cause," she said.

We were starting to get responses to the letters we had sent to our friends in North America. These letters became a life-line for us; each one filled with faith and encouragement. A number of the letters contained checks to help with the expenses of the search and negotiation, and a few stated that their gift could be used for ransom if so needed. Some requested that their gift not be used for ransom. Each donor's wishes were respected.

Patty finally learned to cope with inquiries from the people on the street. She would just say, "You know I can't talk about things like that." That usually put an end to the questions.

Tom's friend arrived at six o'clock the next morning. The letter had been written by a bilingual friend in Villavicencio after consultation with Tom and the missionary. They had taken my advice and advised the guerrillas to accept Tom's offer as he was in very poor health, and, in event of his death, there would be no one with whom to negotiate. In their letter to the guerrillas, they stated that they had reviewed Tom's resources, and they could offer two-and-a-half million pesos and still leave something for the ailing, elderly couple to live on. That turned out to be a mistake. As soon as the guerrillas learned that there was something left to live on, they wanted that too.

I flew the letters out to Chaparral, Chaddy got them to Mapiripan, and from there it was up to the Espitias. When the Kirbys became involved in the negotiation, the Espitias wanted to charge Tom for his share of the expenses involved. The entire operation was fairly costly, involving airplane gas and maintenance, gas for the outboard motors, to say nothing of people's time involved. Chaddy's outboard motor was destroyed during the course of the negotiations; the users were so nervous they forgot to add oil to the gas. However, I did not want to put an added burden on Tom, so our family covered most of the expenses. For this reason I was especially grateful for the help of our dear friends at home.

We eagerly awaited the outcome of this, the fourth contact with the guerrillas. Patty was elated. She felt that Mrs. Kirby's release would be the first step of the fulfillment of all that she had heard from God. Rickey's release would strengthen her faith that Russell would soon be released as well.

Finally the letters arrived. Our note from the captors was encouraging. They had reduced their demand for Russell to 15 million pesos. Off to Villao we sped with Tom's unopened letter. The news was bad. They had rejected the Kirby offer and continued demanding 10 million pesos.

The fifth contact was set for September 30. Patty was thrilled that at last there was a way to send things to Russell. She also took the opportunity to send something to Rickey, gathering toilet articles, books in English, cookies, and other goodies. She even included homemade cinnamon rolls. One of Russell's favorite snacks was a dip made of canned cream and dry onion soup, (he ate it with corn chips), so Patty included the necessary ingredients. As she packed the two boxes, one for Rickey and one for Russell, Patty wondered about the possibility of a mix-up. She couldn't write either name on the boxes. The Espitia brother's greatest fear was that the Mapiripan police would find out we were contacting the guerrillas. Boxes bearing the names of kidnap victims would be incriminating, so Patty explained which was which and left it at that.

I wrote to the guerrillas, telling them that they were in danger of God's judgement, but that God is very merciful, and before a judgment He always gives a warning.

"In the Old Testament of the Bible, when the moment of judgement came for a nation or a city, God sent a messenger or preacher so that the people would know the message of God.

"In the Old Testament these messengers were called prophets. Many times the prophets were prisoners. In most of the cases the people rejected the message of God, and so the punishment of God came, but on other occasions, they accepted the message, and peace and God's blessing resulted."

I told them that their warning would come through Russell and through the letters that we were sending to them.

"Six months ago Russell had a deep experience with God in which he received the message of the Sermon on the Mount. No doubt he has communicated this message from God to all of you. I would like to suggest that the consideration of this message is more important to your group than first appears.

"We are praying that this experience which we are going through will bring each one of us closer to God and to one another. We want the best, not only for Russell, but also for you and for Colombia."

Neftali Espitia returned from Mapiripan on Sunday. He brought three authentic letters composed by Russell—one for us, one for Marina, and one for Chaddy. The guerrillas held firm at 15 million for Russell, but they came down to 5 million for Rickey Kirby. They sent more Polaroid pictures of Russell, and he looked good, even smiling. They had made him a desk of split poles, and it looked like he was doing some writing. He was wearing the T-shirt we had sent him. We noted that his pants were tucked into his socks, so we knew that wherever he was, the insects were bad. Regrettably, there was one disquieting note. The guerrillas had questioned the Espitia brothers about the men who had been sent by Fernando. It sounded like they were furious and were accusing us of sending secret agents.

I flew out to Chaparral with the letter to Chaddy. "There's a secret message in this letter Russell sent me!" he exclaimed after studying it carefully.

"How in the world can you be sure of that?" I responded.

We had all read the letter to Chaddy but did not notice anything out of the ordinary. It was about how to collect some money that people in the *llanos* owed to Russell.

"But those people don't owe Russell any money! It's a secret message!" Chaddy insisted.

We quickly reread the other two letters but could see nothing out of the ordinary. Again we studied Chaddy's letter.

September 28, 1983

Dear Brother Chaddy,

By means of the present, I send you my greeting and hope that this finds you okay. A few days ago I wrote you a letter, but it is only now that they will let me send it. Whatever economic operation you want to do is all right with me. I'm only so-so as far as my health goes, and I hope you settle this problem soon.

I would like to have you do me a favor and collect the following money that people owe me: Carlos of the *Almacen Gigante*[1] owes me 66,690 pesos for motor parts.

Fernando Suarez and Raul Lima also owe me a lot of money, almost a million pesos. Find them and tell Fernando that we are in an emergency.

You won't find Raul Lima in the city but in the old farm of Fernando's. Tell Fernando to take you there so that you can collect the money from Raul Lima. If you can't find Fernando in Villao, look for him at the airstrip with the sheets of zinc where you threw away the torch. Their house is east of the airstrip at the edge of the jungle where the stream starts. Don't look for Fernando at the fish house nor at the lower airstrip.

Whatever you do, find Fernando and have him take you to Raul, so that you won't have problems with Raul's people.

Also, by means of the present, I authorize you to collect all the money that is due me from the fish business. There

---

[1]The name of the store where Russell was captured in Canyo Jabon.

are still 9 or 10 who owe me and I hope you won't let any fugar (escape?).[2]

I feel very useless here, and I can't do anything. I am very tired of being in the jungle so long. I wish you success, although I know it will be hard to get these people to pay.

R. Martin Stendal

"Can't you see!" Chaddy explained. "He is sending me a message that the guerrillas can't understand. They are all happy with the letter because it tells us how to get some money that we can pay them as ransom, but these people mentioned in the letter don't owe Russell any money! He has to be telling us where he is and what to do about it!

"In the first place, look at the amount of money he says Carlos owes him, 66,690 pesos. Remember our family anecdote about the number 6669—666 being the number of the "beast", and 9 standing for final judgement. Here Russell is alerting us that there is a secret message in this letter. He may even be communicating that Carlos betrayed him to the guerrillas.

"A lot of this doesn't mean anything," Chaddy continued, "and is just to confuse the guerrillas, but I know where that airstrip is. It is on an old farm where I threw out a torch once and started a grass fire to clear the strip of high grass. He is telling us where the house is, and where he is being held. I think the next paragraph means that he has nine or ten people guarding him and doesn't want us to let any of them get away."

I thought it all over. It did make sense. I had been expecting Russell to do something to help us. This must be the break I had been waiting for. I decided to figure out a plan to rescue Russell. I doubted that the guerrillas would release Russell to us, even if we paid a ransom. They probably did not want his influence to continue in the *llanos*. He knew too much about their operations. Also, they were asking sums of money that were impossible for us to raise. A rescue seemed to be the only solution. Now that we knew where he was, this alternative needed to be investigated.

---

[2]The word *fugar* in Spanish has the connotation of 'escape.' His use of this word seemed to imply that he wanted his guards all wiped out. However, this was not his intention. The word *fugar* was used to pinpoint a stream, Canyo Fuga. The nine or ten did refer to the number of his guards. He thought that if a rescue operation were being planned, we should know how many guerrillas were involved.

Gloria and Uriel got married in 1984. Sheng (their dog) was the ring-bearer.

CHAPTER 18

The Military Solution

A military solution appealed to many factors in my background. I had been a captain in the paratroopers and an expert marksman. Actually, deep down inside, I knew as a Christian I was supposed to love my enemies. I had gotten to the point where I could pray for Russell's captors, but somehow it gave me great satisfaction to plan out various military rescues. After all the weeks of hopeless frustration, now that we knew where Russell was, I was just the man to do something about it.

After dinner, with the whole family present except Chaddy, we began talking over possible plans to rescue Russell. We believed Russell was being held on the far side of the Guaviare River. After crossing the river at night, Chaddy and I could stay out of sight in the edge of the jungle until we got to the location where they were holding Russell. A half-mile from Russell was a house in the grassland where we believed a farmer's family prepared food for the guerrillas.

I had a high-powered rifle with a telescopic sight, and I hadn't fired on a crack rifle team for three years for nothing. The house was far enough away from the jungle so that a shot near the house would be hard for the rest of the guerrillas in the jungle to hear. I figured I could sneak up in the high grass to about 200 yards from the trail connecting the house and the jungle and shoot whatever guerrilla came for the food. After a while they would send somebody to look for the first man, and he too would be a target. While I was keeping them busy from this side, Chaddy would be locating Russell's immediate guard, and after overpowering or shooting him, free Russell.

"I'll pick them off one by one as they come down the trail," I boasted.

"But what if Russell has been witnessing to them, and now they are Christians?" Patty asked.

"Well, then, I guess I'll just send them straight to heaven," was my offhand reply.

This unfortunate remark didn't seem quite right to Gloria. She thought about it for a minute and finally expressed her doubt, "Yes, but would Daddy go to heaven?"

Something told me I better think this through again.

I was receiving a lot of pressure from my mission and certain other friends to not pay a ransom. However nobody seemed to oppose a military solution. Our whole American TV and movie culture called for such a solution. It was the standard plot of a good man who is wronged by the bad guys and who finally takes the law into his own hands and shoots all the bad guys. I knew how John Wayne would solve this. What I really needed to know was how Jesus Christ would solve it.

The sixth contact with the guerrillas, set for October 4, was upon us. I wrote a letter imploring them to come down from the unrealistic figure of fifteen million. I offered them one- and-a-quarter million pesos. The reaction was not encouraging. They held to fifteen million for Russell and continued insisting on five million for Rickey. Even worse, the letter to Tom Kirby contained an ultimatum: If Tom did not agree to pay the five million pesos in his next letter, the guerrillas would break off the contact.

Patty and I were at the Espitias' home in San Martin, reading the letters and discussing how to proceed. Since Tom had already stated that he could not pay more than the offered two-and-a-half million, the Espitias thought we should withdraw from the Kirby negotiation. It looked like a lost cause, and the brothers were afraid it would jeopardize the negotiation for Russell as well. If the kidnappers got too disgusted, they would just kill their captives, and that would be—The End. The consensus among the Espitia family was that we should take the initiative and refuse to handle the Kirby correspondence. By distancing ourselves from the Kirbys, perhaps we could keep the contact open for Russell. Patty asked them what they thought would happen to Rickey Kirby. In answer, one of them drew a forefinger across the throat significantly.

Something rose up within us in protest. I knew we could not morally withdraw from the Kirby negotiation, even if it would make our chances better to get Russell out. Patty and I were in agreement: If the Espitias wouldn't continue to participate in the negotiation for Mrs. Kirby, we would retire from the negotiation for Russell. This brought the Espitias to their senses, and we all agreed to continue the struggle for the release of both captives.

The idea of the guerrillas giving an ultimatum was very upsetting. We dreaded the day when a letter to us from Russell's captors would contain this word. That night after dark, Patty, Sharon, and I drove to Villavicencio, taking the distressing communication to Tom. We felt very discouraged. We were now offering large amounts of money, and the guerrillas were treating it like peanuts. How were we ever going to get Russell and Rickey out of the guerrillas' hands. If the Kirbys couldn't come up with five million pesos, how were we, a family with much less resources, ever going to come up with 15 million? Patty began to pray earnestly in the dark as we bounced along on the bumpy road. God guided her mind back to the story of the children of Israel in Egypt. She remembered the ten plagues. With each plague it looked like the Israelites would be released, but each time the Pharaoh wouldn't let them go. Our contacts with the guerrillas were somewhat similar. Each time we made our offer and sent the letter off with hope and prayers, but each time the "Pharaoh" said, "No." This emotional roller coaster was wearing us out. Reading each letter from the captors was like plunging a knife into our hearts.

As Patty meditated along these lines, God took hold of her thinking: *Just as the Egyptians finally were so anxious to get rid of the Israelites that they drove them out, even so, the guerrillas will finally be glad to have Russell go. They will want to get rid of him.*

As we drove along in the dark, Sharon and I counseled Patty to say nothing to Tom and his friends about the proposed military rescue. Patty did not agree. She thought it wasn't right to put Rickey's life in jeopardy without Tom's knowledge and consent. Sharon and I thought it was most probable that Russell and Rickey were being held together and would both be rescued.

We felt that secrecy and surprise were so important that no one should be told. Patty brought up the possibility that if they were being held in widely separated locations, Russell's rescue could lead to retaliation against Rickey. We agreed it was possible, but not too likely. We were quite sure they were being held in the same location. The Polaroid pictures seemed to have been taken with the same camera, and the surrounding terrain looked the same.

When Tom read the letter containing the ultimatum, he was devastated. Patty's heart went out to him. In spite of our warnings, she told him there was another possibility and spelled out the proposed rescue attempt. He did not veto our suggestion. We left with the impression that his reaction was: Good, go right ahead and do it.

I tried to think of how to contact the army general in Villavicencio without alerting the guerrillas' spies to the fact that we were dealing with the authorities. I knew that the informers were everywhere. A country person, casually inquiring about his military status at the Army Brigade, could be an informer, reporting to the subversives who it was that came to talk to the army officials. Or the informer could be a secretary in the general's office. I dared not take a chance.

At last we came up with a plan. Uriel was going to the Brigade Headquarters to check up on his draft status. He would take a personal message to the general, asking him to meet me privately in an inconspicuous spot.

Uriel queued up with other teenagers who were working on their military papers. When his turn came, he told the soldier that he had a personal message for the general. This was highly irregular, and the soldier tried to get Uriel to tell him the message. Uriel held firm, so the soldier called his sergeant. Uriel wouldn't tell him either, so finally a captain was called. Uriel kept repeating that his message was only for the ears of the general.

"Don't be difficult, young man," insisted the captain. "I represent the general. Anything that can be told to him can be told to me."

"I'm sorry, sir," Uriel replied, "but my message must be given directly to the general".

"The general is a busy man. He doesn't have time to see you.

He will be very angry if you don't give your message to me first."

"I must see the general," Uriel insisted.

At last, in desperation, the captain took him in to see the general. The general looked up from his work with a puzzled expression. Why was this teenager being admitted to his office? "I come with a message from Chad Stendal," started Uriel.

"Come right in!" cried the general. "Sit down! Won't you have a *tinto!*" He ordered everyone to leave the room and closed the door. A time and place was agreed upon for the general to meet me. When Uriel emerged from the general's office, he was treated with great respect by the surprised members of the general's staff.

Chaddy was now right at my side, helping me in every way. Finally, he was assuming the position of the elder son that had not been possible when Russell was present. It was a real breakthrough in my relations with Chaddy, as we worked and prayed together for Russell's release. Many times the Lord gave Chaddy the necessary spiritual insight to make the right decision that had to be made. I learned to respect Chaddy's judgement. He knew the jungle and the Colombian mentality better than I did.

Throughout all the weeks of planning and working out a feasible plan of rescue, we had considered two main alternatives: Do it all by ourselves, just Chaddy and me and perhaps a few loyal Colombians, or confide in the Colombian Military with Chaddy participating as guide and to ensure Russell's safety.

The general met us the next day in the designated place in Villavicencio. He wore inconspicuous street clothes instead of his uniform. The general was especially cordial and helpful when he discovered that I was a former army officer. One of my hesitancies in using the military was the fear that they might be more interested in destroying the guerrilla unit than in saving Russell's life. After talking with the general, I was reassured that he gave the highest priority to getting Russell out alive.

He said he would put the very best commandos he had on the rescue attempt. He took me to the airborne training center, and they were using all the old, familiar equipment I had used at the Ft. Benning Airborne Training Center back in 1948. What memories returned as I looked at the parachutes being packed and the various training harnesses and mock jump towers. I talked with the lieutenant who was to lead the raid and inspected the equipment and training level of the men. They were as capable as the men I had trained with, and I was sure they would do a good job.

We flew the colonel (who commanded the battalion) and the major (in charge of operations) in the Cessna 170 over the terrain where the rescue unit of about eighteen men plus Chaddy would have to travel. Then Chaddy and I returned to Chaparral and made final plans. Chaddy borrowed a dugout canoe large enough to hold all the men and hid it in a stream in the jungle between the Guaviare River and the grassland about three miles away. The grassland contained an old abandoned airstrip that had been used by drug traffickers. They were not using it anymore, and it was overgrown with grass. Our men cleaned it, checked for potholes and had it all ready for the DC-3 that would land with the troops.

I would accompany the plane to point out the airstrip, and as soon as it landed, Chaddy would take the soldiers into the jungle where the dugout canoe was hidden. The plane would return to the base and at night Chaddy and the soldiers would cross the Guaviare and spend the next two days traveling only at night. When they reached the site where Russell was held, they would have to make up a plan of assault based on what they discovered there.

"If you run into any country people on the way, you will have to take them along with you as prisoners," I heard the colonel tell the lieutenant. They couldn't risk anyone giving a warning to the guerrillas.

Chaddy had been doing a lot of thinking and praying concerning his part in this military operation. He wanted to help rescue his brother, but he was not at all sure God wanted him to kill someone, not even a guerrilla. He seemed to have come to the decision that he would rather die than be responsible for taking another person's life.

Initially, the general had talked about letting the commandos' hair grow out and dressing them in civilian clothes so they would look like country people. Now he had changed his mind and was planning to loan Chaddy an army uniform. When Chaddy heard the instructions about taking prisoners, he really became discouraged. It was entirely possible that they would run into his friends and neighbors. He did not want to be part of an army unit that captured his acquaintances. People throughout the entire region would assume that Chaddy was a spy for the military.

After much prayer and great reluctance, I decided not to personally take part in the military rescue. The Lord had sent me to Colombia as a missionary, and it just wasn't right to bear arms and run the risk of having to shoot guerrillas, no matter what the provocation. I was in Colombia to bring them the gospel, not bullets. On the other hand, the government soldiers were the legally constituted persons to enforce the law. I decided to leave it in their hands. We sent out this letter to our closest friends.

October, 1983

Dear Friends,

My first reaction in regard to ransom was that we should refuse to negotiate and even perhaps issue a statement to the Colombian press that it was morally wrong to pay a ransom. Russell's Colombian wife, Marina, could not understand this attitude and was driven to tears, thinking that we regarded money as more important than Russell's life. To make a statement that we will not negotiate a ransom is equivalent to turning Russell into a martyr, since they will most likely kill him. Do I have the right to do this without his consent, and against the wishes of his wife and her family?

In addition, several members of Marina's family are acting as go-betweens in the talks with the guerrillas. Do I have the right to jeopardize their lives? They have already been threatened with death if anything goes wrong with the negotiations. I should appreciate your opinion. I cannot offer a ransom I do not have. If the Lord supplies it, designated to be used as a ransom or wherever needed, that would help us make a meaningful decision. If the Lord wants Russell to be a martyr, I should be most proud to be his father.

To pay a ransom in itself cannot be wrong, since God

gave His Son as a ransom for us. I also do not believe the problem can be decided in a legalistic fashion, simply saying a ransom is always wrong, since I can find no such Scripture. Each case must be decided individually then, and we are asking your help to decide.

Sincerely in Christ,
Chad Stendal

P.S. We have been praying that God would do something special to favor Russell's release. We decided to leave the question of ransom up to Russell, and we wrote the kidnappers that. We got a reply back from Russell that seems to indicate exactly where he is, in a way the kidnappers would not be able to understand, but which Chaddy was able to interpret. We are now getting ready a rescue attempt. It will involve crossing a major river and three days through the jungle. We will travel only by night as there are at least 70 heavily armed guerrillas in the area.

We request your special prayers. We may have to move everyone, including Russell's wife's family of eight brothers and sisters, most of whom are adults, out of the way of possible retaliation, which will involve a lot of expense.

On the other hand, if we don't find Russell, we shall try to return unobserved, so that we can continue to negotiate for his release.

CHAPTER 19

Marina Faces the Captors

Our spirits had lifted since we started planning a rescue operation. At last we were taking the initiative. We were no longer at the mercy of the whims of Russell's captors. On October 9th, the day before the impending contact, I wrote another letter to the guerrillas. Uriel and Marina checked the Spanish, and Patty typed it. We were now offering 1.4 million pesos for Russell's release. Our hope, however, was now in a military rescue, and not in negotiation. All was ready for an early morning take-off to keep our seventh rendezvous in the jungle with the guerrillas.

At six o'clock the next morning, Tom Kirby's missionary friend was at our door with a letter for the kidnappers. "Tom has decided to sell everything he has and pay the five million pesos for Rickey's release," he told us. "Tom asks that you put the rescue attempt on hold until he is able to get Rickey out of the guerrillas' power."

It was with mixed feelings that I carried Tom's letter out to Chaddy at Chaparral to be given to the Espitias who would take it upriver to the guerrillas. I was delighted that Rickey's release was likely, but disappointed that the military operation would have to be put on hold. Now it seemed that we were back to square one again.

The next day we got a radio message from Mapiripan. It seemed the guerrillas wanted to meet with Marina. They had set the date for October 12, which was the following day. I was to fly Marina to Mapiripan as soon as possible, and her brothers would take her to meet the guerrillas in the jungle. It would be our eighth contact with the kidnappers.

The next morning Marina stepped into a dugout canoe with her brothers. She was terribly nervous. Her brothers confided that each one of these trips upriver was an ordeal for them. The mood of the Communist negotiators was unpredictable, and it was disconcerting to be surrounded by men with submachine guns pointed right at them. Their only motivation to endure such agony was their desire to secure the freedom of their sister's husband. Marina's stomach was tied in a knot, and she was trembling visibly. She knew that Russell's life and hopes of freedom depended on her wisdom, choice of words, and self-control in this encounter.

Later, Marina told us that as the motorized dugout canoe slowly progressed up the broad, swiftly-flowing river, she imagined that the eyes of subversive sentinels were watching from the thick jungle foliage along the shores. Her mind wandered back over her three years of marriage. Having been raised a devout Catholic, she had a strong desire to please God but had trouble relating to Him. When she had first met Russell, she had noticed something very different about him. It was his personal relationship with God that had attracted her to him. From the very beginning of their courtship and marriage, Russell was very careful to base their union on a proper relationship with God. Marina developed a relationship with the Lord through Russell. She took her problems to God through Russell and received spiritual direction from God via her husband. Now Russell was lost to her, and her connection with God was obstructed as well.

In her distress that morning, her heart reached out to the God that she had experienced together with Russell. She began to silently call out to Him for strength and wisdom in this difficult assignment before her.

After traveling some two hours more, the brothers took out a large piece of red flannel and covered the outboard motor. They explained to Marina that this was the sign ordered by the guerrillas. They continued slowly upstream. They were now in guerrilla-controlled country; thick jungle bordered the river on both sides. Marina was trembling all over. Suddenly, some fifty yards ahead of them, a man waved a red piece of cloth from the end of a pole.

The canoe beached at the point indicated by the flag. The man holding the flag ordered, "You get out," indicating Marina, "and the rest stay in the canoe."

Marina got out alone, and the guerrilla led her back into the thick jungle where a group of guerrillas stood. One was obviously the commander, and two guards stood near him, their automatic weapons aimed at Marina, and their fingers on the triggers. Among the guerrillas in the group, Marina noticed that one was a woman, and one an Indian. She could hear the sound of others, out of sight in the heavy foliage. All were heavily armed.

"You know that this is a kidnapping to raise money for our revolution, and you know how much we are asking for your husband," the commander stated.

To her surprise, Marina found that her fear was gone. She had stopped trembling and spoke in a firm, steady voice.

"Well, you kidnapped the wrong person then, because we don't have forty million, nor ten million, nor five million. We don't have any money.

"You people know everything, and you should know exactly what the Stendal family has. Russell works to support me. You know what they do. They help the poor; they help people. Just

Neftali Espitia (Marina's father) and Baby Lisa. The strain and worry of Russell's kidnapping shortened his life.

because they have an old airplane and a homestead and are *gringos* does not mean that they have money."

Marina felt a supernatural power to speak up with confidence. She tried to play on the leader's sympathy and reach his heart. She told him he should be ashamed of himself for kidnapping people and causing their families such anguish. She told him that Lisa would be having her first birthday in a few weeks, and she wanted Russell at home. She ended by asking him how he would feel if his wife or mother were kidnapped.

The leader wilted a bit under Marina's verbal attack. Marina noticed that the guerrillas behind the leader were struggling to conceal their emotion. At least one had tears in his eyes. The leader rallied and defended himself by saying that while the kidnapping had not been his decision, all his men were always totally in agreement when operations like this were undertaken.

"What is the matter with this man then?" Marina asked, indicating the one with tears. If you are always in agreement, how come some of your men have tears in their eyes? Maybe you have them intimidated and here against their will too."

At that the leader softened a bit and tried to comfort Marina saying, "Your husband will miss your daughter's birthday this year, but there will be other birthdays."

The leader then turned to questioning Marina about the two men who had been sent by Fernando. They had made contact with Russell's captors about three weeks earlier. It was soon evident to Marina that a terrible misunderstanding had developed concerning the negotiation for Russell. At this time the guerrillas were demanding 15 million pesos, and we were offering 1.4 million. Fernando's contacts offered 20 million pesos, supposedly authorized by us. (They thought this was a considerable reduction from the original guerrilla demand of 40 million pesos. After all, my parting words to Fernando had been, "Try to get them to reduce their demand.")

Even though placed in such a difficult situation, Marina maintained her composure. She felt a supernatural power to speak up with confidence. She told the commander that we were telling the truth in our letters and that we had never authorized Fernando's men to offer 20 million. She assured the guerrillas that we had no 20 million to give them. She explained that these men had been sent as an attempt to find out what had happened to Russell, since it had taken so long to hear from the captors.

The guerrillas set October 20 as the next contact date and told Marina she had to return and give a better explanation about Fernando's friends. They set another ultimatum for Tom Kirby. They wanted the five million pesos by October 25, or else. . . .

CHAPTER 20

Lisa's Ordeal

Friday night Patty and I returned to San Martin from Bogota. Gloria told us that on Wednesday night baby Lisa had been very sick with fever and vomiting. Since Marina had gone to talk with the guerrillas, Gloria and Clemencia, Marina's younger sister, took Lisa to the local hospital where they gave her an injection to stop the vomiting, ordered a malaria test, and released her. Lisa seemed better in the morning, and since both Gloria and Clemencia were afraid of needles themselves, they decided not to take the baby for the blood test to avoid the trauma of the needle prick. That night she was sick again, but now they didn't dare take her back to the hospital because they had ignored the doctor's orders for the malaria test. When Marina returned, she concurred with Gloria and Clemencia's decision despite the fact that Lisa continued to have vomiting and diarrhea.

When we arrived Friday night, Lisa was asleep so we retired as well. In the morning when Marina carried Lisa out of the bedroom, we almost fainted. The plump, healthy baby that we had left on Wednesday, was now a shadow of her former self: pale, thin, and listless, with huge circles under her eyes. Since the girls all agreed that we couldn't take her to the hospital again without the malaria test, Patty took her to the laboratory. The visit was traumatic, as by now the baby was very dehydrated, and the nurse had to draw the blood from the jugular vein, but in a few hours we received the results of the test, and it was negative.[1]

Patty and Marina then took the baby back to the doctor at the hospital. A woman physician prescribed some liquid medicine for Lisa and sent her home. But by now, Lisa was too sick to keep the medicine down.

To continue this story, I need to share a little background. When Russell and Marina got married, Patty knew that Marina would have customs different from ours and determined to be an understanding and tolerant mother-in-law. Patty had not been with Marina much since Lisa was born and did not yet feel enough confidence to give Marina advice.

Saturday night was dreadful for Marina. Lisa continued to be very ill. She was dehydrating and losing strength rapidly. Marina, emotionally fatigued from so recently confronting the guerrillas, felt desperate. She felt that she had probably lost her husband and was now in danger of losing the baby as well. Furthermore, Marina felt that she was not receiving spiritual and emotional help from us. She became aware of the barrier that existed between her and her mother-in-law. 'These people talk about God, and how He has done miracles of healing in their ministry. *Why aren't they helping me?*' Marina wondered.

She had been up three or four times to check on the baby in the crib. Instead of fussing as before, Lisa now lay white and still. In her exhaustion, Marina placed Lisa on the double bed beside her and tried to sleep.

Marina's thoughts turned to Russell. He had explained to her that he had made a total commitment of his life to Jesus Christ and had told her that he wanted her to make the same type of commitment. She dozed off for a few minutes but was awakened by a noise. To her horror, Lisa had fallen off the bed onto the floor. She appeared to be dead.

Frantically, Marina gathered her baby into her arms, held her up to God, and started to pray. "Lord, don't take my baby too! It seems like I have lost my husband; don't take my daughter too! Take charge of our lives! I don't have help from anyone else; I authorize you to take charge of our lives!"

In another bedroom an anguished Patty was still suffering

---

[1]Since malaria is so prevalent in the *llanos*, the doctor wanted to rule it out before making another diagnosis. Laboratory tests in San Martin are done in a private lab, unconnected with the hospital.

from the fear of being a meddling mother-in-law, and so was waiting for Marina to ask for help.

The next morning it was evident that immediate action had to be taken to save the baby. Marina did not have confidence in the local hospital because so many people had died there, so we decided to start for Villavicencio, which had a much larger facility. Uriel went to get the Toyota. It was an unusually cold day for San Martin. Once about every four years a strong cold wind blows up from Brazil, lowering the temperature in the llanos to way below normal. This was the day. Uriel came in to tell us that the Toyota was malfunctioning. The engine had quit four times between the garage and the house.

Of course we had been praying for Lisa, but as Marina was wrapping up the baby to go to the hospital, Patty suggested that we all lay hands on Lisa and pray. Marina readily gave her consent. Working with the Kogi Indians for many years, we used this approach to sickness often. We would pray for the patient, then treat him medically the best we could. God honored our practice and the hundreds of sick people that I prayed for and treated all recovered. We firmly believed that medicine can be given, but in the last analysis, only God can heal. When the person was healed, we always thanked God publicly. There are other factors which play a part as well, such as the patient's will to live and faith in God.

Patty was suffering mental agony because she had not taken more forceful action right away when she first returned from Bogota. What if Russell returned from the jungle and found Lisa dead? What would we ever say to him? We had never expected the child to get this sick. Now Patty thought it was a distinct possibility that we would be stalled on the road in this unusual cold, and Lisa would die before we could get help. All of a sudden she spoke up forcefully.

"Our only hope to save this baby is to take her back to the hospital here in San Martin! We have prayed to God, and now we have to trust Him that the doctors here will have wisdom to treat her correctly."

Marina agreed, and off we dashed to the San Martin hospital in the unreliable Toyota. The same young woman doctor was on duty. At once she realized the gravity of the situation, hospitalized the baby, and ordered an I.V. started.

We had her put in a private room—bare except for the hospital bed and a small, bedside table. Patty went home and got a reclining lawn chair for Marina to sit in. Lisa was completely unaware of her surroundings. She lay completely still, her small, pale form lost in the adult-sized bed. At midnight Patty went to the hospital to replace Marina. Lisa still lay completely still, her left arm taped to a wooden board to receive the I.V. fluid. Patty dozed a little in the reclining chair. All of a sudden, about 6:00 A.M., Lisa opened her eyes and let out a scream. Patty was at her side in a moment. She looked at her left arm and started having a fit at being restrained. Luckily at that moment in walked Marina, who was able to calm Lisa. We knew now that she was over the crisis. She would live.

When Patty arrived back at our house after spending the night with Lisa, we realized that this was the day Dr. Ware was due to arrive. Dr. Ware was the Mission Board Chairman of one of our principal supporting churches in the States, and he was visiting various missionaries that his church supported in Colombia. We were to meet him in Villavicencio.

Patty and I kept our appointment with Dr. Ware. Patty thought the title, Doctor, probably indicated that he had a Ph.D. in missions or theology. She started to tell him about Lisa's illness, and to her surprise, he said that he was a medical doctor in family practice.

Dr. Ware offered to see the baby, even after hearing of the deteriorating security situation in the llanos. On the way we discovered that he had grown up in Cuba, the son of missionaries. His family had lived through the Communist take-over in Cuba, and he was most sympathetic with our situation.

Back at the hospital we found Lisa was about to be dismissed. Her bill was only 1,000 pesos or $12.50.

At our house, Dr. Ware examined Lisa and told us that she had received very good care in the hospital. He looked over her prescriptions and made a few minor changes, then I took him back to Villavicencio, rejoicing in the way God had answered our prayers by giving the hospital staff wisdom in treating Lisa, and even bringing a medical specialist all the way from Seattle.

On the way back to Villavo I asked Dr. Ware, "Were you in Cuba during the revolution?"

"Yes," he replied, "I was only fifteen at the time. The Communists fired without warning from ambush at my parents on two occasions. The second time they wounded my father badly, and then we all left Cuba. My father tried to tell business and professional people, among others, what would happen if Castro took power, but they said that a revolution was just what the country needed."

"I wonder what those people would say now?" I asked. "Have you heard from any of them?"

I was astonished at Dr. Ware's reply. "A good many of them are in Miami. After the Communist take-over when all businesses were confiscated and all freedoms were lost, they began to realize how wrong they were. Over a million people left for Miami. A great many perished by firing squads and thousands are still in jail."

Dr. Ware indicated that conditions now in Colombia looked just like those in Cuba before the Communist take-over.

CHAPTER 21

Trouble Dead Ahead

The next Wednesday I had to fly Marina back to Mapiripan for our ninth contact with the guerrillas. Each of these flights was about one hour long over jungle and grassland. We were just entering that very dangerous time of the year when the seasons change from rainy to dry. Unusual weather could be expected and violent storms were very common. Strange downdrafts and wind shears complicated landings and takeoffs.

The 1952 Cessna 170 had never let us down. Oh, it had its little eccentricities, but we managed to stay on top of them. About every hundred hours the valve guides on the two back cylinders would carbon up and had to be cleaned. A little gas filter on the carburetor would plug up about every 30 hours, and the gasoline had to be filtered because of the water that it often contained.

The old gutless wonder (145 h.p.) had one big advantage going for it. It had a big open-throated carburetor instead of the fuel injection system that newer planes had.

Fuel injection is a great system in the United States. It gives fuel economy and works well in cold weather, but in the tropics it's murder, literally. Just one drop of water will stop a fuel injection system, and in the jungle where gas comes out of fifty-five gallon drums, heavy with water condensation, an open carburetor is much better. Several times over expansive jungle, the little Cessna 170 had coughed and wheezed when water passed through it, but after several uncomfortable moments, it would start up again and keep going.

125

Chaddy accompanied Marina and me on this flight to Mapiripan, and at first everything went fine. I knew every stream and river, every opening in the trees, and so it was easy to navigate our way onto the mighty Guaviare River. The wide, winding river could be seen from many miles away. Below us were the beautiful rolling hills, alternating with dense jungle and open grassland. Here and there cattle were grazing. Occasionally a clearing was cut in the jungle, indicating a homesteader or Indian was living there. The Indians made round clearings, and the colonists always made rectangular clearings, so it was easy to tell them apart.

However dead ahead was trouble. A squall line was pushing clouds up from the stormy, rainy area below, and thunder and lightning were occurring right in front of us. A very black line of clouds was almost touching the ground. Even Chaddy, who always appears cool and unconcerned, looked worried. "What are you going to do, Dad?" he wondered aloud.

Marina was looking at the problem and gave her advice immediately, "Let's go back!" That was wise advice, and ordinarily I would have turned back. But if we missed this critical appointment with the guerrillas, the whole negotiation might fall through. I had to take the risk.

"Fasten your safety belts! I'm going to try to get through underneath. If I fly at treetop level, I should be able to maintain visual contact even in the rain." I just barely put the plane under the deep black cloud, when the turbulence grabbed the plane and jolted it violently up and down at about fifty feet at a time. All the dust and loose items on the floor of the plane ascended to the ceiling and then back again. Marina screamed and tried to grab me and the wheel in a panic. Chaddy held her, and I quickly got the plane turned around.

"Boy, Chaddy, that was a tough situation! Another few seconds and the plane would have been torn apart!" I exclaimed.

It was all Chaddy and I could do to calm Marina down, especially when she found out that instead of going home, I was trying to maneuver around the side of the storm. We managed to work around the storm, going off course almost twenty minutes, with Marina bawling me out all the way. Finally we rounded the corner on the storm, and I could set a course for Mapiripan once again. A rainbow appeared. "See that beautiful rainbow, Marina? I told you everything would be all right." We landed at Mapiripan in light rain, with nightfall closing in on us. Every flight in the jungle is an adventure.

In Mapiripan I stayed overnight with Raul, Marina's brother. The town had many guerrillas mixed in with the townspeople. Since the guerrillas didn't wear fatigues or carry weapons in town, it was impossible to tell who they were except when they were actively causing a problem. They were in the process of eliminating anyone who opposed them. At night the police were afraid to leave their quarters, and shots and screams were a common occurrence. In the morning sometimes, bloody spots were visible on the ground, but the bodies had disappeared. People told us of seeing the guerrillas dragging bodies or screaming victims to the river where the bodies were carried away and probably eaten by the fish. No one dared report anything they might have seen to the police for fear of retaliation by the guerrillas.

Fortunately, having landed in the rain, no one seemed to notice my arrival. After an anxious night, sleeping in a hammock in Raul's house, I wasted no time in rushing to the airport, getting the plane off the ground, and heading back to San Martin.

The next day Marina went upriver with her brother to meet with the guerrillas. They wanted the twenty million that had been offered through the men we had sent through Fernando. Marina had a difficult time trying to convince them that yes, we had sent the men; but no, we had not authorized them to offer twenty million. And furthermore, we did not even have twenty million pesos. In regard to the Kirby negotiation, instead of the 25th, they set October 26 as the day to release Rickey Kirby in exchange for the five million pesos that had been agreed upon.

On this same day, while Marina was in the jungle meeting with the guerrillas, the telephone rang at our house in San Martin. A man's voice asked Chaddy to meet him at the *Oriental*, an ice cream parlor in San Martin. The *Oriental* consisted of one long, dark, narrow room with many tables, each seating four people. As is the custom in Colombia, the ice cream parlor served more beer and *tinto* than ice cream.

Main Street in San Martin. The jeep is in front of the *Oriental*.

At the *Oriental* Chaddy was met by Alvaro Garcia, a swarthy, middle-aged Colombian from Villavicencio. He was one of the two men who had been sent by Fernando. He had just returned from his encounter with Russell's kidnappers and presented Chaddy with a dictated letter from Russell dated October 18, two pictures of Russell with the Bible, and a note from the captors. They were now asking for a ransom of thirty million pesos. Chaddy told Mr. Garcia that we didn't want to deal with him at all. We preferred to continue the jungle contact with the Espitia brothers.

October 25 was Lisa's first birthday. Russell and Marina had been planning a huge party to celebrate. Now with Russell kidnapped, Marina still felt that Russell would want us to have a party. Patty baked a birthday cake, and most of Lisa's eleven uncles and aunts, plus grandparents and other assorted relatives and friends, were present. We all tried to be cheerful in spite of the dismal state of the negotiation. We were tremendously thankful to have baby Lisa in our midst, albeit still a bit thin and pale from her illness. We thought of Rickey Kirby's family and friends, and hoped that they were able to make their deadline the next day. How we detested these ultimatums.

CHAPTER 22

Chaddy Disobeys Guerrilla Orders

October 26 dawned bright and clear. At an early hour, Tom's missionary friend arrived in his jeep, bringing with him a young woman friend of Tom and Rickey's who was entrusted with carrying the ransom to the captors. Lydia was an energetic Colombian woman, completely bilingual and extremely brave. She was the wife of the American who had been writing the letters for Tom. With her she brought a duffel bag containing five million pesos in Colombian currency. (At that time the largest Colombian bill was one thousand pesos, so the bulk of five million pesos was considerable.) She laughingly told us that she had included a change of clothes and some personal items in the duffel bag in case they decided to keep her, too.

Our immediate problem was to load the airplane and avoid being searched by the local police who frequented the airstrip. We would be in danger of losing the money or at least having it impounded. A suspicious-looking green vehicle was parked a block away from our house, and the driver appeared to be watching us. We were probably being watched either by the government secret service or the guerrillas' agents. We decided to have the jeep that had brought Lydia leave our house, drive by the suspicious car, and keep going in the wrong direction to confuse the watcher, while we, with Lydia and the money, headed straight for the airport by a route that was out of the sight of the green car. I had made friends with the police guarding the airstrip, but I was very apprehensive as I greeted them, carrying the duffel containing five million pesos over my shoulder like it was my personal effects. They didn't challenge us, and we loaded the plane.

I flew Lydia out to Chaparral and left her with Chaddy. We couldn't take her to Mapiripan because the police there would search the incoming passengers and find the money. Lydia and the money would have to be moved at night past the police checkpoint on the river. This was no easy maneuver either.

Lydia was visibly worried about the long trip upriver in the dugout canoe, past Mapiripan to the rendezvous with the guerrillas. Five million pesos would be too much temptation for almost anyone in that area. Chaddy had sent a message with the Espitias on the October 20th contact, asking if he could be along on the next contact. The guerrillas' reply was an unequivocal "No!" They said they didn't want to see him under any circumstances, not even in a picture. We learned later that Russell had told his captors many stories stressing Chaddy's jungle expertise and popularity among the people of the *llanos*. All was true; his aim was to discourage them from accepting Chaddy as their captive in exchange for himself. Russell was afraid that Chaddy would find captivity so restrictive that he would take unwise risks to escape and probably be shot. Russell's strategy had worked. The guerrillas didn't want to see Chaddy, not even in a picture, which is a common Colombian saying.

But when the time came to get into the canoe and start upstream, Lydia refused. The only one she knew and felt she could trust to protect the money was Chaddy. "I'm not going to go unless Chaddy comes along," she emphatically stated.

Raul Espitia insisted that the guerrillas would be angry if more than three people arrived in the dugout canoe. The only ones approved to go were Raul, the person bringing the ransom money, and the man who operated the outboard motor.

"Then I'll replace the motor operator," decided Chaddy.

He pulled a baseball cap down over his blond, curly hair instead of his usual cowboy hat and hoped he would not be recognized.

When they arrived at the rendezvous point, Chaddy left his gun under some boards in the bottom of the canoe, tied the canoe to a tree, and stayed at the river's edge. Meanwhile, Lydia and Raul were escorted some twenty yards into the jungle to talk with the guerrilla leader. Raul had brought a letter from me to the *captores* stating that we did not want to negotiate through Alvaro Garcia in Villavicencio.

For some reason the guerrilla leader did not open the letter but demanded that Lydia tell him what it contained. This really put Lydia on the spot, since she had not seen the contents of the letter. She turned to Raul, but he had not read the letter either. She was so nervous that she blurted out, "Maybe Martin's brother would know."

At the word 'brother,' the commander turned his attention for the first time to Chaddy, who was making himself inconspicuous at the river's edge.

"Are you Chaddy?" he shouted in rage and amazement.

At that Chaddy came over to the area where the others stood.

"*¡Si, a la orden! ¿En que puedo servirle?* (This is the customary polite greeting in rural Colombia, roughly translated, "Yes, what can I do for you?")

The commandant had been in a bad mood to start with, and now he was really angry. "You were told not to come here," he roared. He was not accustomed to having his orders disobeyed.

Chaddy stood his ground, calm and unintimidated. He explained that he had to come to accompany Lydia and the money. "Did you want the money to arrive safely, or didn't you?" he demanded.

The leader backed down a bit and started questioning Chaddy about the contents of the letter. He was incensed at my reluctance to deal with Alvaro Garcia in Villavicencio.

"Why doesn't your father want to negotiate with him?" he demanded of Chaddy.

"Because he doesn't trust him," responded Chaddy. At this the commander became even more furious. "Are you saying you don't trust us?" he shouted, jabbing Chaddy in the stomach with the barrel of his assault rifle.

"I said we don't trust the connection from Villavo; we want to keep this contact here in the jungle," replied Chaddy.

"If you don't trust the contact in Villavo, you don't trust us. We're all the same," the guerrilla insisted, emphasizing his point by jabs with the gun barrel.

"My dad doesn't trust the contact in Villavo," Chaddy

calmly continued. "You people are in a business negotiation with only one buyer. You would be wise not to antagonize him. My dad doesn't like to negotiate with you, and if he refuses to deal with you at all, then what will you do?"

Hearing this unexpected challenge, the leader began perspiring and trembling with rage. He had expected Chaddy to be cowed into meek submission by the rifle in his abdomen. Instead, Chaddy held the commander's eyes in a defiant, unblinking gaze.

The two men stood about a foot apart, the gun barrel still jammed against Chaddy's stomach. Our son was silently praying. He finally realized that the guerrilla leader was tremendously agitated and that it was not wise to push him any farther. He looked away, and as soon as Chaddy broke the eye contact, the guerrilla took a step backward, as though relieved that the crisis had passed.

The commander consulted with another guerrilla for a few minutes and then he turned to Lydia. "Did you bring the money?" he asked.

Lydia beckoned to Chaddy, and he returned to the canoe. Realizing that five million pesos would be very bulky, the guerrillas expressed concern about where it was hidden. To their amazement, Chaddy picked up one of the two outboard motor gas tanks. All the guerrillas came out of the brush into the little clearing where the leader was standing to see what was happening.

Chaddy reclimbed the steep, muddy bank to the clearing and tossed the gas tank into the middle of the assembled guerrillas. "Here's your money!" he announced.

The subversives scrambled for cover like scared rabbits, while Chaddy stood there grinning. "What's the matter, don't you want your money?" he asked.

"Is this some kind of a joke?" the leader grimly queried. The guerrillas had thought the gas tank could be a bomb.

Chaddy borrowed a machete from a guerrilla and pried the bottom off the gas tank, revealing the neatly stacked piles of one thousand peso bills.

"Do you certify that it is all here?" the commander challenged Chaddy.

"To the best of my knowledge," replied Chaddy. "I have not

counted it myself, but the bank says it is five million."

"Are there any counterfeit bills in there?"

"If there are, it is the fault of the bank. The money is just as it came from the bank."

Chaddy had dumped the money out of the gas tank onto a plastic tarp. The leader looked at the stacks of bills and estimated that it could be about five million pesos. The guerrillas were intrigued by the ingeniousness of hiding the money in the gas tank. They asked for the gas tank, but Chaddy refused. Gas tanks were hard to come by in the jungle; he would reweld this one and keep on using it for gas. Several guerrillas wrapped the money up in the tarp, making a neat package of it, and carried it off.

Now it was Chaddy's turn to be disconcerted. It seemed like he and Lydia sat there a long time. The guerrillas now had the money, but there was no sign of Rickey Kirby. One of the guerrillas seemed to be trying to convince the commander that he should hold Chaddy captive. "No, a deal is a deal. They would never trust us if we did that," he heard the leader say. To diplomatically divert their attention from that train of thought, Chaddy asked about Mrs. Kirby.

"She'll be here in a little while," the leader answered. "I hold you responsible to keep her out of sight for two weeks, so we can cover our tracks. If her release comes to the attention of the authorities before the two weeks are up, your brother will pay the consequences.

"We have not had an easy time with the *Señora* Kirby," he continued. "She is very strong-willed and difficult." The commander's tone showed a grudging respect. "I'm sure glad to get her off my hands; I wish you luck with her." And then as an afterthought he added, "Have you any idea how ornery she is?"

"I know what you mean; I've dealt with her in the past," Chaddy gravely replied. At this comment, the guerrilla smiled in spite of himself.

After awhile, Raul caught a glimpse of Rickey coming slowly through the jungle. He silently motioned to Chaddy and Lydia. The delay had been due to the fact that she did not believe she was being released. "Just more of your lies," she was telling her guards.

This was the third time Rickey had been brought to the

rendezvous point. When Marina first met with the guerrillas, Rickey was back in the jungle waiting to be released, but the ransom money had not arrived. Now she was irate at being brought to this area again. She was moving slowly and making as many problems for her guards as possible.

When she reached the clearing, she saw Lydia and gave her a big hug. Then she turned to give some last choice words to the guerrillas, and her eyes lit on Chaddy.

"What are you doing here?" she exploded.

It seemed to her to be the last straw to see Chaddy Stendal with the guerrillas.

"Well, I came to take you home, Mrs. Kirby," Chaddy answered with a smile. At that she gave Chaddy a big, big bear hug.

While Rickey was hugging him, Chaddy was signaling Lydia and Raul to get into the canoe. He wanted to make a fast exit.

"Do me the favor of greeting Russell for me," were Chaddy's final words to the commander.

He took Rickey by the arm and carefully helped her down the steep, slippery bank. From the canoe Lydia called to her, asking how she had been treated by her guards.

"Most of them were O.K.," responded Rickey, "but see that one over there?" Her voice dropped to a loud stage whisper, "He made life difficult for me. Something should be done about him."

"You should have heard what he said about you," commented Chaddy.

"What did he say about me?" she asked.

"Oh, he said that you were strong-willed and ornery."

"Oh, he did, did he!"

Chaddy caught her by the arm as she started to climb back up the bank. "Leave well enough alone, Mrs. Kirby," he said.

"I was just going to give him a piece of my mind," Rickey replied.

The foursome traveled downstream. It was still too early to take Rickey past the police checkpoint in Mapiripan, so after awhile, they stopped and waited until dark.

Rickey did not know that Russell had been kidnapped until Chaddy told her. She had been held in a completely different part of the jungle, upstream on the Guayabero River, a tributary of the Guaviare.

The guerrillas had told Chaddy and Raul that they were definitely terminating these contacts in the jungle. It had been the tenth encounter. From now on, the negotiation would be handled by Alvaro Garcia in Villavicencio.

After the darkness had fallen, they let the canoe drift silently downstream with the current, passing the police checkpoint on the far side of the broad river.

Meanwhile, I waited at Chaparral for Chaddy to return with Mrs. Kirby. As the night wore on, I became more anxious. Did Chaddy make it through with the money? Did the guerrillas release Rickey? About 10 o'clock, the party finally arrived. I hurried over to give Rickey a big hug. She looked much older than I remembered.

In the course of the ensuing conversation, I expressed the thought that one good result of the dual kidnapping was that, as Christians, she and Russell had had a good chance to witness to the guerrillas both in word and conduct. I soon wished I had never said that, as poor Rickey just hung her head and said, "Well, I sure failed. I kicked them, threw mud at them, and made life as miserable for them as I could."

Little by little, she told us of various incidents that must have exasperated her captors. They told her to cover her head whenever they passed another canoe on the river so she would not be recognized. She did just the opposite and dropped her shawl whenever they passed another canoe. When the guerrilla leader said something she didn't like, she gave him a hard elbow in the ribs, and on one occasion threw mud at him. The guerrillas didn't know what to do with her, and finally they threatened her with a hangman's noose, implying certain death if she continued to misbehave.

Chaddy and I were both chuckling over the problem the guerrillas must have had with Mrs. Kirby, as she recounted tale after tale of her exasperating acts. The one I liked best occurred on the Fourth of July. The guerrillas were having a big indoctrination meeting with some ranking leaders and left Mrs. Kirby with a single guard. She convinced him that she was making a study of ferns, and soon the two of them were down on their hands and knees investigating ferns. Little by little, Rickey inched herself closer to the political meeting. After getting into a good position, she suddenly jumped up and shouted, "*¡Feliz Cumpleaños a los Estados Unidos de America! ¡El unico pais en donde hay verdadera libertad!* (Happy Birthday to the United States of America, the only country that has real liberty!) The Communist leaders were furious, but Rickey felt good all week.

On thinking it over, I don't think Mrs. Kirby failed in her testimony at all. Her brave, indomitable spirit of freedom in the face of their submachine guns must have left a memorable impression on the guerrillas.

At no time did she seek to buy their consideration by pleading or acquiescing to their demands that she write letters begging help. With the Lord's help, she showed no fear—however, she may have felt. She did not expect to get out of that situation alive, but she did not hesitate to express her opinion of their organization and aims, yet she never forgot to say thank you for a small kindness.

Even though the commander had told Chaddy that we should keep Mrs. Kirby hidden for two weeks at Chaparral, threatening retaliation against Russell if we didn't comply, I decided to take her back to Villavicencio immediately. Rickey had been through so much, and her sick husband was anxiously waiting to see her. She could stay out of public view there for the two weeks.

The next morning dawned bright and sunny at Chaparral. We lifted off in the Cessna 170, and I headed for Mapiripan so that Rickey could see her ranch from the air for the last time. Imagine her emotion as she looked down on the ranch house, the corrals, and rolling green grassland. Some twenty-five years of her life lay below her. She now knew that the ranch and cattle had been sold, and that she would never again ride the range she loved so well. I could say nothing to console her as the tears fell from her eyes. She stared at the ranch as long as she could still see it, as we continued on to San Martin.

CHAPTER 23

A Secret Weapon

In order to keep Mrs. Kirby's return a secret, we whisked her past the police guards at the San Martin airport with a shawl over her head. They were used to having us bring sick people in from the jungle and thought she was another one. Fortunately, she wasn't recognized. She spent her first day of freedom resting in one of our bedrooms, chatting with Patty, who was delighted to have Rickey here in our home at last. It was the tangible fulfillment of the Lord's word to her when Gilberto had first brought the bad news of the kidnapping. It strengthened her faith that Russell would soon be released as well.

Rickey told Patty all the details of her months in captivity, and most of it was reassuring. It was, however, discouraging to hear that she had been forbidden to talk to her guards, except for brief, necessary communication. She had not been allowed paper nor writing instruments. 'How is Russell going to be a witness,' we thought, 'if he isn't allowed to speak or write?'

"I was treated like a valuable animal," Rickey told Patty. "I was fed fairly well and cared for physically, but the guerrillas had no regard for my feelings or my mental and emotional well-being."

"What would have happened to you if the ransom had not been paid?" someone asked.

"They would have gotten tired of me eventually and shot me," Rickey stated matter of factly.

Rickey confided to Patty that several years before she was

137

kidnapped, she had encountered God in a personal way.

"Shortly before I was kidnapped, I had asked the Lord if there wasn't some way I could have a six-month Bible course," Rickey recalled. "When the guerrillas tied me up and threw me in the back of my Toyota, I kicked and struggled for all I was worth. But when I realized that my kidnapping was inevitable, I asked if I could please have my Bible and my reading glasses.

"Several of the girl guerrillas were sent into the house. They found one of my old suitcases and packed a few clothes. My reading glasses and a New Testament were on a small table by my bed. They brought my glasses, but instead of the New Testament, they looked through my bookshelves and brought my big Thompson Chain Reference Bible. This was the only book I was allowed to have during almost seven months of captivity. I had my six-month Bible study all right," Rickey stated with a wry grimace, "but it wasn't exactly what I had in mind! I read that Bible through and through, including the notes and the footnotes."

"There happened to be the stub of a pencil in the old suitcase," Rickey continued, "and between sections in the study Bible were blank sheets of paper. By being very careful that my guards not catch me writing, I was able to keep something of a diary."

Patty asked about the English books she had sent to Rickey, but none had been given to her. As might have been expected, the items in the packages sent for Russell and Rickey had gotten mixed up. Rickey had received the canned cream and had been told it was sent by Tom. Patty told her about Russell's chip dip.

"That explains something," chuckled Rickey. "We have never used canned cream for anything except to eat with strawberries. I knew Tom would never send me canned cream. If by some chance he should, he would have sent strawberries too, so I accused my guards of being liars for saying that Tom had sent the cream, and if not, they were thieves for stealing the strawberries. Now I know why they looked so bewildered!"

That afternoon while Patty and Rickey were still talking, Sharon returned from the United States. She had called many of our friends, giving them first-hand news of our situation.

Patty's brother-in-law, Ralph Burton, in Minneapolis had been researching tracking and homing devices and had been able to get one. He inserted the small transmitter in the metal frame of a fairly large backpack. This devise, used to plot the migration of ducks and geese, contained two lithium batteries, a tiny transmitter, and a 10-inch flexible woven-wire antenna. It had a range of about 25 miles and a battery life of more than six months.

The backpack frame was made of hollow aluminum tubing. The battery and transmitter together were about two inches long and about the diameter of a dime. They were inserted in the hollow left vertical support, right at the "T" made with the upper horizontal support. The antenna extended into the upper horizontal tube. To take the frame apart, Ralph had to cut through the original rivets and then re-rivet it in such a way that it showed no signs of being tampered with. There was no way anyone could find the "bug" without sawing up the frame in little pieces.

The receiver was more bulky and consisted of a box about the size of a portable radio. The antenna was about a foot long and looked like a small television antenna. This could be attached to the airplane. If we could get the backpack to Russell, we could determine his exact whereabouts, which would greatly aid the rescue attempt. But, I wondered, how would we ever get the backpack to him?

Rickey was not encouraging when we told her about the planned rescue attempt. She warned us not to underestimate the capabilities of the guerrillas. After dark, Lydia arrived in her jeep, bringing Rickey some clothes and cosmetics, and took her to Villavicencio where she would remain secluded until the time stipulated by the guerrillas had passed.

I was anxious to get on with the military operation now that Rickey was safely out of the guerrillas' hands, but Chaddy felt that Russell was no longer in the place he had indicated in the letter. "I'll go if you want me to, Dad," he told me, "but I feel in my spirit that he has been moved."

What a sad turn of events that would be, I thought. Would all Russell's ingenuity of communicating his location to us be lost because of the delay? It was just too distressing to think about. I imagined Russell's anguish as they moved him away from the spot where he had hopes of being rescued. A possibility occurred to me: if we could get the backpack in Russell's hands, we could fly over the spot Russell had indicated and try to pick up the signal. Then we would know whether they had moved him.

The next day Chaddy received another call from the *Oriental*. Alvaro Garcia wanted to meet there with Marina.

Since her last encounter with the guerrillas, Marina had become extremely distressed. Before then, it had seemed as though the negotiation had been proceeding as well as could be expected. It had also seemed obvious that the guerrillas wanted to terminate the Kirby case before coming down to realistic ransom figures for Russell. They had promised Marina and her brothers that, if they cooperated in handling the communications concerning the Kirby negotiation, the captors would in turn cooperate by bringing Russell's case to a speedy and favorable conclusion. It had seemed only a matter of time—first Rickey, then Russell would be liberated. Now with the sudden change in the negotiation Marina's hopes were shattered. Instead of a ransom demand of 15 million and lowering, we were now faced with a doubling of the guerrilla demand. Marina was completely disheartened. She did not have the trust and confidence in Alvaro Garcia's willingness to struggle for Russell's safe return as she had in her own brothers. She wanted no part of negotiating with Alvaro Garcia.

We all shared the same anxiety, but we had the military option and the "bug" to sustain our hopes. We had not felt that we could safely divulge either of these two developments with Marina. At one point, we had asked her if we could trust her to keep a secret from her family. She tearfully responded in the negative, explaining that she had to have the freedom to communicate everything she knew to her father and brothers.

We, in turn, felt that the success of these two projects depended on complete secrecy, and we could not risk leaks by bringing more people into the plans. Colombians feel that the only way out of a kidnapping is with a negotiation and the payment of ransom. In contrast, Americans always think of direct action, based perhaps on our background of "westerns" and war stories. The good guys go in and take back that which is rightfully theirs.

In addition to the struggle between Russell's family and the kidnappers, there existed a minor struggle between those of us who were playing major roles in the scenario of getting Russell back. Some pressed for paying ransom, while others argued for a rescue. In the final analysis, the responsibility for the right decision was on my shoulders. I could only look to God for wisdom in making the right choice.

CHAPTER 24

The Guerrillas Are Outsmarted

Chaddy found Alvaro Garcia drinking a *tinto* in a far corner of the *Oriental*. He had brought a letter from the *captores*, as the guerrillas called themselves. For the first time the dreaded word, "ultimatum" appeared in a message to us. They were asking 30 million pesos, but no date was set as a deadline.

"Can you believe it, Dad?" Chaddy exclaimed when he returned to the house. "I am to meet Alvaro Garcia in Villavo tomorrow with a letter containing your offer and an article, that will be photographed with Russell to prove that he is still alive."

"Do you suppose that we can get them to take the backpack?" I questioned.

"I don't know. It's pretty big, but we can certainly try," Chaddy responded.

Ralph had filled the backpack with items from the United States that would be useful to a person out in the jungle. Any one of them was distinct enough to serve as the item to be photographed with Russell. We had to remove these and fill the pack with items purchased locally. Nothing could be distinctive except the backpack. Otherwise, Alvaro Garcia would only send the smaller item and leave the backpack.

Marina helped me draft a letter to accompany the backpack, part of which read as follows:

October 29, 1983

Estimados Captores,

It seems strange to me that you have kidnapped a person with such modest resources. I am thinking that maybe there is another reason that we don't know. Maybe we have done something that you don't like. If this is the case, I want you to tell me, so that we can do better. We have tried to do good in the community, and I don't believe we have any enemies ... We have helped many people regardless of their political ideas or religious beliefs.

We have received a letter asking 30 million pesos. Before, you asked 15 million, and we offered 1.4 million. What is happening? Are we dealing with the same group? We have had ten contacts with you. We have sent many documents—income tax declarations, letters from the bank, titles etc. Did you receive these, or are we dealing with new people who know nothing of the previous negotiations?

Your leader who talked with Marina, Russell's wife, said that if we helped with the case of Mrs. Kirby, this would help in the recuperation of Russell. We have done our part, and now you are asking twice as much as you were before. Marina is very sad about this. If you won't keep your promises, how can we keep negotiating?

We are sending a blue backpack with articles for Russell. You can take a photograph of him with the backpack to prove he is alive.

The statements in this letter to the guerrillas were designed to put them in a defensive position in the negotiation. We hoped this would cause them to accept the backpack, as I was demanding assurance that they were the same people who had Russell, and that he was still alive. I began to realize that we also had quite a bit of leverage. They had Russell and were asking a high price for him, but we were the only buyers!

The next morning Chaddy and I took off for Villavo in the old battered Toyota jeep. Chaddy was to meet Garcia at his restaurant that afternoon, alone. I began to worry about Chaddy's safety. What if they somehow found the "bug"? What would they do to Chaddy? I decided to go first to the Intelligence officer the general had set up as a contact for us. This army captain listened to what we had to tell him about the coming contact.

"I'll have two of my best plainclothes agents stake out the restaurant, so nothing goes wrong."

"Be sure they are not seen, or the guerrillas may break contact with us," I cautioned.

The captain reassured me, "Don't worry! These men are experts and do this kind of thing everyday." I still had lingering doubts, but I thought we had at least secured a little safety margin for Chaddy.

About four o'clock in the afternoon, Chaddy left me off in the market place and drove alone to the restaurant to meet Garcia. In the back seat was the backpack with the "bug" hidden in it.

I looked about the market, waiting anxiously for Chaddy's return. Hours went by, and I became more and more apprehensive. I ate supper, and still no Chaddy. Finally it got dark, and everybody went home except me. I began to imagine all the possible things that could have gone wrong. Had they found the "bug?" Had they spotted the secret agents? Had they taken Chaddy away with them?

When 9 o'clock came and went, it was clear something had gone drastically wrong. I decided to go to see the army captain. By means of his two secret agents, he should be able to tell me what happened. Fortunately, I was able to find the captain at that late hour. He knew nothing.

He, in turn, rounded up his two agents, and the story they had to tell was not reassuring. The captain had said, "Keep an eye on the backpack," and so the agents thought that they were supposed to watch the backpack instead of Chaddy. They had seen Chaddy leave the restaurant about 4:15, but they kept their eyes on the backpack, and Chaddy went out of sight. At 6 o'clock, when their duty shift was over, they went home.

The captain was furious. "Here we had a chance to make contact with some *bandoleros* (bandits), and you guys blew it!" He criticized the agents at length, while they looked at their toes in silent embarrassment. The whole affair began to look like "Get Smart" a TV spoof on espionage. Maxwell Smart and Agent 99 couldn't have messed it up better.

Quickly I returned to the market where I had agreed to meet Chaddy. My heart beat faster when I recognized the red Toyota parked where we had agreed to meet. But where was Chaddy?

The jeep appeared to be empty. However, in the darkness of the back seat, there was Chaddy, sound asleep. "Boy, Chaddy, you really had me worried!" I exclaimed. "What happened?"

Chaddy slowly woke up, and his story unfolded: "Well, it developed that some of the guerrilla leaders from the jungle were in town and wanted to see me. To make sure I wasn't followed, they sent me from one place to another, all over Villavicencio. As I reached each location, someone would give me another address to go to. I suppose they were watching behind me to see if any government agents were following. After several hours of this, I was able to meet the leaders. I don't know what happened to our government agents, but it is sure a good thing they didn't follow me."

I explained what happened to the two agents, and we both began to realize that what appeared to be a foul-up on their part, was really very fortuitous for Chaddy. I might even say providential. We realized God was looking out for Chaddy and we then decided to trust Him in the future, and not rely on a Laurel and Hardy pair of secret agents.

One thing I was still dying to know. "Did you get the guerrillas to take the backpack to Russell?"

"Yes, but it wasn't easy! We had to return to the jeep, and as soon as the man they sent with me saw the backpack, he said only half jokingly, 'That looks like it's got a "bug" in it.' I tried to stay calm and replied, 'Rip it apart if you want to.'

"The man carefully examined the pack. Ralph had done a good job, and he could find nothing suspicious. 'It's too big to take along,' he complained.

" 'You can put it inside a piece of luggage,' I told him. As he still hesitated, I finally said, 'Look! You're the ones that asked that we send something along to photograph with Russell. You can refuse to take it, if you wish, but my father is getting upset with the way you are conducting this negotiation—changing negotiators and upping the ransom. If you don't take this with you, I don't think he will negotiate anymore with you.' With some hesitation, he took the backpack."

An important factor in their taking the backpack was Chaddy's wonderful ability to make friends with Colombians. I have no doubt he was able to put everything on a congenial basis. His humble simplicity must have impressed the guerrillas. This was no son of a rich American. This was a man of the people, just like them. I am sure this, together with Marina's intercession, influenced the guerrillas in our favor for the rest of the negotiation.

Having gotten the "bug" into guerrilla hands, we knew that they would have to go through the Villavo airport to catch a plane to their destination in the jungle. To narrow the search area, it would be helpful to know what town they flew to. So we took the aerial and receiver and went over to see Jaime Gonzales, our radio technician friend. Jaime took the aerial and receiver to the airport. He aroused no suspicion there, since he regularly worked on airplane radios at the airstrip. He was able to pick up the signal transmitted by the "bug," as the guerrillas' man walked through the terminal to his plane.

Jaime's round face beamed with delight as he heard the characteristic beep-beep on his earphones as his antenna pointed to a man carrying a big, white suitcase, presumably with the backpack inside. Jaime was a hundred yards away, and everyone thought he was checking out radios. Jaime just loved being in the middle of all this intrigue. If I were Don Quixote, fighting impossible battles in this melodrama, Jaime would be my Sancho Panza.

CHAPTER 25

"El Pito, El Pito"

Every day brought encouraging mail from our families and friends, and also from those whom we didn't know personally, but who wrote to say they were praying for us and for Russell. Many shared Bible verses they said God had brought to their attention, especially for our situation. About this time a letter arrived from Chicago from a couple we had never met

> . . .We have been praying for Russell's release and have spread the need for prayers among our Christian friends. On September 10 we were in prayer and devotion, and the Lord laid upon my heart a prophecy regarding Russell. The enclosed copy of the prophecy does indicate that Russell will be released. We don't want to raise your hopes unnecessarily, but we do feel that this is of the Lord. Several other prophecies of this nature given to me these last few years have proven to be accurate and were fulfilled.

Enclosed was a sheet with the text of the prophecy:

> He will be released; he will be freed unharmed, for I have called him to serve Me. I will use him to call my people to repentance. I have a great reward for him, both on earth and in heaven. For I will use this suffering for a purpose, and it will in no way be as great as the reward I have for him.
>
> I will use him to serve me, and my power and love will be manifested through him. I will go forth before him and lead him.
>
> So do not fear, my little ones, for I have called this thing

to pass for a purpose. It will glorify My name before the whole world. It will brighten the darkness, for there is much darkness there, and it must not prevail. My light shall and must go forth. Don't you know that I have control of all things, and that this thing is not difficult for me?

But you must trust, and you must be obedient. You must not fail to give me glory and to credit my name with this release, for it will come to pass.

With the negotiation in such a dismal state and the military operation uncertain, it was hard for me to believe that everything would turn out all right. Deep down in my spirit, I felt that Russell was going to come out alive, but at this point I didn't know if by negotiation or military intervention. At the same time, all outward evidences were indicating disaster. I was experiencing a conflict between mental reasoning and inward faith.

I had read accounts of various types of family trials, including kidnappings and abductions, and the consensus was that these crises frequently tore families apart. Personal recriminations, inter-family conflicts with one family member blaming another for what had happened, often resulted in divorce and life-long estrangement among family members. Damaged relationships even occurred in cases where the abducted family member was released unharmed. The Lord had clearly shown me personally, that if Russell was to come out alive, I would have to walk in the Spirit, listening to the Lord's voice, and do exactly what the Lord wanted done every moment of every day. As head of the family I had the additional responsibility to try to secure that every other family member do the same.

Because of the change in the negotiation procedure using Alvaro García and Chaddy, instead of Marina's family, a new possibility for conflict and misunderstanding arose. I called the whole family together for prayer and explained how all these pressures and trials very often destroyed a family. I insisted that it was absolutely essential that our family maintained its unity and love, no matter what trials or tragedies lay in the future. With blunt honesty, I noted that it was entirely possible that we could lose not only Russell, but several other family members as well. Everyone in the family made a special commitment to walk as closely as possible to the Lord, realizing that Russell's fate hung in the balance. We each pledged to one another that these trials would bring our family closer to one another and closer to the Lord, instead of tearing us apart.

Now that there had been time for the backpack to have been safely delivered, we needed to check up on Russell's whereabouts. Without attracting suspicion, Jaime Gonzales was able to ascertain the destination of the plane carrying the backpack. It was a regular commercial run to Mapiripan. Since this was the closest air service to the location Russell had indicated in his letter, I was encouraged to believe that maybe they hadn't moved Russell after all, and we would be able to go ahead with our plan.

Fidel, the mechanic, and I carefully installed the aerial on the top of the right wing of the airplane, so that when the plane was directly over the transmitter in the backpack, the wing would momentarily block out the signal because of the radio interference of the aluminum wing.

Several people watching this installation at the San Martin airstrip snickered to one another, "That *gringo* must have a TV set in his airplane." I just smiled and let them think that. It was better to have them think we had a TV set in the plane than to realize we had a homing capability. We had already synchronized the frequency of the "bug" with the receiving devise, and they worked fine together.

Chaddy, Jaime, and I took off, flying over the green, rolling hills mixed with jungle, to Chaparral. As we passed the various winding, muddy rivers that we knew so well, we could hardly wait to get to the point where we could start listening for the beeper. But first we had to land at Chaparral to gas the plane and check on conditions at the ranch.

We suspected that one of the ranch workers had been intimidated by the guerrillas to inform on our activities. He would report the coming and going of the plane, but I knew they would not attack us now. They wanted us around to raise the ransom. They assumed we were looking for a needle in a haystack, since there were thousands of square miles where Russell could be hidden. They had no way of knowing that now we had the capability of going directly to the needle, like a magnet.

It was one year ago to the day, that the guerrillas had fired so many bursts at our airplane as I was taking off from the fish house airstrip. Now the fish house was closed down; the honest work that it had given to so many people was now gone. Some in their desperation had now gone into planting coca (for cocaine). It was still very traumatic just to land the plane in this area where I had been shot at. Even though I assumed they would leave us alone at this time, I never really knew if somebody was going to open fire at the edge of the airstrip with automatic weapons.

We took off from Chaparral with great anticipation. Chaddy was in the co-pilot seat, watching every detail on the ground, and Jaime, the radio man, was in the back seat like a child with a new Christmas toy, as he put on the earphones and experimented with all the settings of the homing receiver. We headed straight for the spot where we thought Russell was being held. We were hoping that Russell was still there, and we were trying to confirm that by picking up the signal. Jaime was straining to pick up the first faint beep.

As we neared the location our expectancy increased. I turned to Jaime as we passed over the site. He shook his head, and with that all our hopes were dashed. We continued out and made passes over the whole area. Still there was nothing. Finally with our gas running low, we were forced to reluctantly return to San Martin where Patty and the girls were eagerly waiting, trusting that we would return with Russell's location secured. It was so painful to dash all their hopes.

The next several days produced more disappointing flights over different areas of the vast, vast jungle. We found nothing. All we could see for hundreds of miles was endless jungle—and we heard no beeps. The rounded tops of the huge rain forest trees looked like an ocean of broccoli from the air.

November 3 was my 56th birthday, and after flying futilely all day, I returned home totally depressed. Patty had made my favorite pie, lemon meringue, but even it couldn't lift my spirits. It was tasteless in my mouth. All I thought about was our failure to locate Russell.

I tried to relax from the strain of the extensive flying by reading our recent mail, but it was hardly relaxing. Some well-meaning friends had written and advised us not to pay a ransom because they knew of two recent kidnappings where a ransom had been paid, and the victims had been killed anyhow.

Guayabero Indians on the Guaviare River on their way to a Christian conference at Chaparral. Some of these Indians later helped us look for Russell.

We weren't the only ones in Colombia going through this type of ordeal. In the same year that Russell was abducted, there were several hundred known kidnappings and thousands of unreported kidnappings, extortions, and killings in Colombia. In the cities, key businessmen, journalists, and politicians were being assassinated at an alarming rate. Those who opposed the subversion were being systematically eliminated. A common method of assassination was to hire hoodlums who would pull up alongside a selected businessman's car on a motorcycle. The man on the backseat of the motorcycle would pull out a compact machine gun from his leather jacket and fire directly at the victim from very short range. Another favorite method was to hide behind the bushes and shoot the man with a shotgun as he stepped out of his door on his way to work in the morning.

The country was suffering a great trauma and crisis, and we were suffering with it. Our prayers were now prayers of desperation.

The next day Jaime arrived from Villavo eager for another flight. I could hardly face another day of disappointment, but there was always the hope that this day might be different. We had now systematically covered the entire area where we thought Russell was being held for fifty miles in every direction and farther on the rivers. But we just couldn't raise a peep out of our homing device. Knowing that in addition to this flight radius, we had a receiving range of another 25 miles, it did indeed seem hopeless. We had now eliminated all the area north, east, and south of the ranch Chaparral, and were proceeding west along the Guaviare River, making large, ten-mile "S" turns on either side of the river. We proceeded upstream to the point where the Ariari River and the Guayabero River join and form the Guaviare. We continued up the Guayabero River until we could see the start of the *Raudal*.

The Guayabero had its beginning high up in the mountains. As it left the mountains, it continued flowing slowly across a large, jungle plateau. At the end of the plateau, a huge, impenetrable escarpment fell to the level of the lower jungle and impeded the descent of the river. This rocky ridge, several miles in width, extended at right angles to the Guayabero, which was now a large, major river, for miles in both directions. The *Raudal* was a spectacular, roaring drop between high rock palisades. It was a twisting, unnavigable collection of rapids and waterfalls.

We entered the canyon at low altitude in an upstream direction. The tropical afternoon sun was making rainbows in the immense spray. Dugout canoes had to be portaged on a steep trail, sometimes hacked out of the rock. All three of us were speechless with the immensity and beauty of the scene below us. As we reached the top, the water was flowing towards us calmly again. The huge river and the high plateau extended as far as we could see. We were now over territory completely controlled by the guerrillas. If they had brought Russell up here, it would incalculably complicate a rescue.

Behind us the area was still mostly under the control of the Colombian government, even though the guerrillas were trying hard to assume power. Before us now lay an area completely dominated by the FARC. Here the FARC ruled supreme. Here was an independent totalitarian state within the democratic republic of Colombia. The dugout canoes and launches moving on the river below belonged to guerrillas or guerrilla sympathizers. I had not flown over this area for several years, and I was astonished to see the tremendous build-up of farms and coca fields (for cocaine).

As we flew mile after mile up the Guayabero River, I was keeping a careful eye on the fuel gauge. A forced landing in this area would be disastrous. Even if we survived the crash, we would certainly fall into the hands of the guerrillas. When we had only five more minutes of fuel before I would have to turn back to San Martin, I looked back at Jaime. Once again he shook his head. Nothing. It seemed impossible that the guerrillas would have moved Russell so far, past police checkpoints and the great cataract and waterfall of the *Raudal*. It appeared we were on a wild goose chase, and I decided to turn around and head home for San Martin. Right at that moment Jaime exploded in jubilation. "*¡El pito! ¡El pito!*" he shouted. *El pito* is what Jaime called the beep beep. With those big black earphones, he looked for all the world like a happy Mouseketeer.

Jaime passed the headphones up to me, and soon we were zeroing in on Russell's location. The signal stopped, and we were directly above the backpack. I was now just one thousand feet away from my son, whom I hadn't seen for months. Chaddy, Jaime, and I celebrated in the cockpit like we had just struck the motherlode in a gold rush. Chaddy and I had never been closer than at this moment that we had worked so hard together to bring about. We continued on flying a little in a straight line, so as not to attract attention from the people below. Then we proceeded full steam ahead for San Martin with the happy news for the family, praising the Lord and wondering if Russell had recognized the distinctive sound of the Cessna 170. We were trusting that the backpack and Russell were in the same location, since the guerrillas had promised to send us pictures of Russell with the backpack as proof that he was still alive.

The next day, November 5, Chaddy met Alvaro Garcia in Villavicencio. He gave us letters that had been brought in from the jungle where Russell was held captive. There were four this time, three in Russell's handwriting, and one from the *captores*. One was to Marina in which the guerrillas allowed Russell to express his love and his regrets at having missed Lisa's birthday party. This was an act of human kindness on the part of the captors. Surely they had been touched by their encounter with Marina.

The letter I received sounded like it was written partly by the guerrillas and partly by Russell. They had forced Russell to copy a prepared letter. Halfway through, he must have realized it was my birthday, because instead of copying the last paragraph containing the usual threats from the guerrillas, he wrote instead: "I wish Dad a happy birthday, and I am very thankful for all you are doing for me." This touched my heart greatly, as he had no way of knowing what I was doing, but he had faith that his father would do the best he could for him. The guerrilla leader didn't notice the change until he had traveled with the letter too far to return. He was very angry, but it was too late to go back and have it changed.

The third letter was for Chaddy. It included pictures of Russell with the backpack, and in the letter Russell said:

> They just gave me a blue backpack with a few things to eat inside. I believe the backpack is going to be very useful to me because they have been moving me all around in this jungle. I'm not sure where I am, but there are a lot of mosquitos here. My shoes rotted, and I need to have you send me some more.

The letter then went on to tell Chaddy to borrow money in his name and get him out of there.

"I'll bet he knows that bug is in the backpack," chuckled Chaddy. "Listen to this! 'I believe the backpack is going to be very <u>useful</u> to me.' He knows something is going on."

Chaddy also noticed that when Russell wrote something with which he agreed, his handwriting was neat. But when the message was something he did not want to say, he wrote with a scrawl, crossed out parts of words, and made spelling errors. By paying careful attention to his handwriting we could better understand what he was really trying to say.

The letter from the *captores* was very depressing. They were still asking thirty million pesos ($375,000 dollars) and had set a deadline of December 3.

Santa Marta
Cienaga
Mamarongo
(Kogi Indians)

COLOMBIA

Bogota ★
● Villavicencio
Caño Jabon
● San Martín
Guaviare River
Sierra Macarena
Ariari River
Chaparral
Mapiripan
Guayabero River
Canyo Jabón
Fish House
Russ's last location
Raudal
(rapids)
Russ first held here

CHAPTER 26

Help from England

That which we dreaded had happened. We now had a deadline, and a completely impossible amount of money being demanded. The next day we wrote letters to the FARC, trying to get them to back off from their unreasonable demand.

Señores Captores,

We greet you, hoping that you are in good health.[1]

I wish to remind you that we helped you in the case of the *Señora* Kirby. Also we have written many letters to which you have not responded. We are tired of writing letters and getting no answer. It seems that, although we tell you the exact truth about our financial conditions, you doubt our word. . .

When you kidnapped the son of missionaries, you made a mistake for several reasons: 1. Our resources are very modest. 2. We do not fear death because we love and trust our Lord, Jesus Christ, and we believe that if we die we go to reign with Him.

If you had kidnapped any other member of our family except Russell, who has a wife and child, we would not have negotiated with you. As it is, we are receiving a lot of pressure not to negotiate in order to avoid future kidnappings in Colombia. We do not have 20 million, nor 10 million, nor 5 million. If you want to negotiate in low figures,

---

[1] In Spanish tradition, letters all start and end with a courteous greeting, in spite of the grim subject with which they may be dealing.

pobremente[2], as you said the day the *Señora* Kirby was freed, okay, we'll negotiate. We can offer 1.5 million pesos, which for us is a lot of money. It's not our fault that we don't have more. Or do you think it is a felony to be poor?[3]

During the Great Depression, my father was out of work. Nevertheless, he tried to support us, selling bread and milk house to house. Even this was difficult because the customers didn't always pay. In those days the government offered help to the poor, but he said, "I would rather die of hunger than receive something from the government for not working." We too would rather die than give one peso to you if you are not going to keep your promises and work for the good of Colombia.

Maybe you don't know that it was I who, with much effort, convinced Tom Kirby that you were reliable and that he could be sure you would keep your side of the negotiation.

> Without animosity,
> Chad Martin Stendal

Chaddy also wrote to the FARC. His letters are not the type a foreigner to Colombia would write. The guerrillas would notice right away that Chaddy was primarily Colombian in his expression and manner of thinking.

Cordial greetings, wishing you well,

I want to ask you a question: Have you ever looked up at the sky, or wondered where man originated? Doing either of those two things, you will arrive at the same conclusion. There is something hard to understand about both—one has no beginning, and the other has no end. In the case of the origin of man, the best scientists say that over thousands and thousands of years, by means of an evolutionary process, man was formed from a microbe. I ask, "And where did the microbe come from?"

When we look up at night, stars can be seen. Beyond those that we can see, we suppose that there are more. But then I ask, "Beyond those, what is there?"

---

[2] Poor, i.e., in the manner of poor people.
[3] I am using this phrase in irony, as this is a favorite expression with the Communists: *¿Es un delito nacer pobre?*

Well, I don't know what you think, but to me it is obvious that there is something here very much out of the normal. Here in this world where everything has its beginning and end, why do we have these two examples so obviously to the contrary?

After studying this honorably, I have become convinced that a God exists. I also discovered that the love of God is without limits. God offers pardon to the one who repents and asks for it. I know that this step is hard and difficult to take, but take heart, don't be cowardly. Repent and ask God for forgiveness, for He won't leave you in a bad condition, and you will be completely happy and blessed.

I tell you this with love, and at the same time, I offer you my friendship. Anything else that you want to know on this subject, ask Russell. He will be able to explain it to you, or look for me in Chaparral.

Now in regards to the negotiation: In the first place, I can guarantee that my dad does not have much money. For my part, I can give you all that I have if you believe that you need it more than I do. We can set a date, and I will turn it over to you anywhere you say. Concerning Russell, it would be good if you would let him go.

I know how you feel because I have lived all my life in the wilderness. I also know what it is to flee from the law, but thanks to God, all this has come to an end. It is not easy to repent of the bad that one has done, but it is necessary in order to be able to understand life.

Honorably,
Chaddy

And to Russell he wrote:

Esteemed Brother,

Receive my greeting. Here are the shoes you asked for, together with a bottle of insect repellant.

I want to ask a favor of you. Share the message of the Sermon on the Mount with your captors. If you have already done so, do it again, explaining it better. This is very important. I believe it is the reason for your being where you are. This is more important than money, or your life, or mine. As soon as you have done as much as possible in regards to this, write and tell me the result. In the meantime, I assure you, we are not going to see any kind of a solution in your case.

I don't know, but it seems like they still don't realize the danger that they find themselves in. Explain it to them with patience, because they, too, have the right to know the truth. Also you can tell them that it still isn't too late for them to be forgiven; all they have to do is to repent before God.

I am offering them all my personal possessions if they need them more than I do. This is not in exchange for your freedom. Also if they want, I offer to go and replace you. Take advantage of these circumstances to give a constructive example, not destructive, regarding the truth. If you can do me this favor, I will greatly appreciate it.

> With love,
> Your brother Chaddy

Chaddy knew the guerrilla leaders would carefully read this letter whether or not they decided to deliver it to Russell. He took the letters and the shoes to Alvaro Garcia in Villavo to be sent to the guerrilla camp, and I got in the plane and went out to listen to the "bug" again. It cheered me considerably to know that Russell was down there with his backpack, sending me little beep-beeps. It was a special tie to Russell that the Lord had provided to encourage and give faith to both of us. I was sure he would recognize the sound of the plane and know I had located him. But we were up against the ultimatum. We had less than a month to go.

Encouraging letters from outside Colombia continued to arrive. Literally around the world, people were praying for Russell's release. Not one person wrote and said that God had shown them that Russell would be killed. Still, I knew that the decision was in God's hands. I could not assume that it was God's will that Russell should live. In this age of comfort and prosperity Christians have lost sight of the fact that to be a martyr is God's highest calling. It should not be sought after, but it should not be avoided in a situation where God calls us to be faithful unto death.[4]

---

[4]"They overcame him (the Devil) by the blood of the Lamb and by the word of their testimony, and they did not love their lives to the death." (Rev. 12:11).

God required me to be willing to have my own son be called as a martyr for Christ and the Gospel. This was a very hard decision to make, but once I had made it, God then gave me the assurance that Russell would come out alive, if I would walk in the Spirit and seek His will. Many years ago God had shown me that to walk in the Spirit meant to be sensitive to God's guidance, even in the smallest decisions of life.

A very interesting letter arrived from a woman in England. I had met her and her husband at the airport in Bogota about a year before. Our daughter, Gloria, who had been studying in San Martin by correspondence, was going away to Minneapolis for her last semester of high school. I noticed a nice, friendly-looking young couple and approached them to ask if they would befriend Gloria should she need help purchasing her ticket in Miami. They said they would be glad to look after Gloria. She sat with them on the plane, and by the time they arrived in the U.S., they had become friends and had exchanged addresses. Gloria's new friends were very interested in South American Indians, so Gloria added them to our mailing list to receive our periodic letters from Colombia.

Now, to our surprise, the young woman wrote saying that her husband was a specialist in representing the families of kidnap victims in negotiating with the kidnappers. He was in Germany at the moment but would be getting in touch with us as soon as possible.

A few days later his first letter arrived. It seemed like an unbelievable miracle to have contact with a person who was actually experienced in cases like this.

We were appalled to hear the dreadful news of Russell's kidnap . . . We have been thinking of you very much . . . and you have all been very much in our prayers.

I think my wife told you I have considerable experience in kidnap negotiations, having done several and being in the process of writing a book about the whole business of kidnap. I am placing particular emphasis on negotiating the safe release of the unfortunate kidnapped person, as I find both families and authorities alike are struggling when so much happens, so many important decisions have to be taken, and all so subjective, being under pressure by people out of your control. I so wish I could have had the book written and merely send you a copy! However I have put together a series of notes which I hope will be of some help. . .

Objectives of the gang: to wear down family determination; etc. Be quite clear that all the threats and horrors they lay on for you are done with this sole intention in mind. All their communications (threats, letters written by them or "written"—usually dictated—by Russell, phone calls, etc.) must be taken with a pinch of salt, with bluff in mind. Do *not* believe anything they say on face value; analyze *everything* from *THEIR* point of view, from *THEIR* perspective. I can't stress this angle enough. Additionally choose a steady manner of negotiating, with the patience of God, for then, whatever they throw at you, they will find your attitude steady, and this makes the whole negotiation, however traumatic for you, safer from Russell's point of view. An erratic approach by a family may be fatal.

I'm sure you're right to pay to get Russell back.

You devote a lot of space in your letter to the question of mounting a raid on the bandits and releasing Russell that way. If you know exactly where he is, then maybe there is a chance. If you plan to carry out a raid, then you should have sufficient men, automatic weapons, and be prepared, if necessary, to kill the opposition—they won't hesitate to kill you. I sympathize terribly with your motives in this area but would advise caution, unless you have the kit and confidence to "get stuck in" to the bandits. It is worth pointing out that hostage release should really be the most surgical of military/police operations.

I am ready to do a more detailed analysis, if you can give me the facts.

We praised the Lord that such an expert on kidnapping as Mark Bles was giving us the benefit of his extensive experience and was interested in our situation. Patty immediately wrote him a letter, outlining the details of our negotiation up to this point and sent it to England. We eagerly awaited the reply.

CHAPTER 27

Rescue or Ransom

The joy of positively locating Russell had so encouraged us, that we tended to lose sight of the tremendous difficulties that were still before us. From the giddy heights of exaltation at the miracle of finding Russell, we were now forced to descend to sober reality. The rescue would now have to be a helicopter operation.

Patty felt very mixed emotions over the idea of a military operation. On the one hand she felt that Russell had indicated in his letter to Chaddy that he wanted a rescue attempt, and we thought we understood that he wanted his captors completely wiped out. We got this idea from his use of the Spanish word, *fugar*[1] (don't let them escape). On the other hand it bothered Patty greatly that Marina had not been consulted. On November 7, she wrote to friends in the United States:

> I feel very torn up over the decision to let the army undertake a rescue attempt for several reasons:
>
> (1) If this rescue attempt provokes Russell's death, what would we ever say to Marina? We haven't been able to discuss it with her beforehand because of the need for complete secrecy.
>
> (2) We would be putting Chaddy's life at risk too, as he is to guide the rescue party.
>
> (3) A young lieutenant, who has successfully completed three years fighting the guerrillas in another part of the

---

[1]Russell was tipping us off to the name of the stream he thought he was on. He was not instructing us to wipe-out his captors as we erroneously thought.

country, is being recalled from leave to lead this mission. He was scheduled to be married in two weeks. I can imagine that his fiancee is not too happy with this development. We would be risking his life as well as those of all the other soldiers.

(4) We will be responsible for killing many guerrillas. In one sense you might say they asked for it, but on the other hand, the Lord has told us that one of the reasons for this kidnapping is to give a testimony and opportunity for salvation to the guerrillas.

Yesterday Chaddy had another meeting with the contact. They are still asking 30 million and now have given an ultimatum and set a deadline of Dec. 3. It could be that they will simply break off this contact, or it could be a death threat.

The next day I wrote a letter that was duplicated and sent out to our mailing list.

November 8, 1983

Dear Friends,

Not long ago I wrote you an urgent letter requesting prayer for a dangerous rescue attempt. We appreciate your prayers. We had located Russell's exact location and were about to move in when Chaddy felt in his spirit that the Lord was telling him that Russell had been moved. At that moment the guerrillas offered to take Russell's picture with any kind of identifying object that we wished to send. Through the picture that returned and through methods I cannot disclose at this time, we were able to establish that Russell was moved to the central headquarters of the guerrillas in a separate mountain range in the jungle. It reminds me of the Apostle Paul who was moved to Rome so that he could witness there as well. . .

People have asked us to state plainly what we want done in regard to a ransom. All we can say is that we want the Lord's will to be done. As far as the kidnappers are concerned, they want the money by Dec. 3, or else presumably they will kill him. We would need $70,000 dollars in addition to what we can presently raise to ransom Russell. We are not asking anyone to send ransom money. However we want everyone to understand that we are entering a final and crucial phase. Any funds given will be used exactly as you designate.

Sincerely in Christ,
Chad Stendal

A few days later, we sent out another letter asking that on November 25, Russell's twenty-eighth birthday, friends join us in special prayer that Russell be restored to us and his wife and daughter.

On November 13, Chaddy was called to Villavicencio again and was given a letter from the captors, written November 10.

Señor Chad Martin Stendal

Appreciated *Señor*: In regards to the business at hand, you now know our last request. You know the amount and the time we are giving you—until Dec. 3, 1983. We can't understand how, since you are intelligent people, you don't understand that this is an *ultimatum*.

From now on we will not do any other negotiation. We have given proof of our seriousness in the business at hand, and this time also we demonstrate how serious we are. We beg you not to send so many letters. All that is needed are those that deal strictly with the business at hand.

You talk of pressure to not negotiate. That doesn't matter to us. At any rate if this pressure exists, we think it's because you have not been sufficiently cautious.[2]

So then, over these last concepts we will continue negotiating.

Cordially,
The Captors

I was in Bogota at the time. Marina wanted me to sell Russell's apartment, but the title was still in the name of the former owner, and there were other problems that made it impossible to sell. Neither was it possible to sell the farm, the San Martin house, or any other possession. There was so much instability

---

[2]Here the guerrillas were warning us to be more secretive about the negotiation.

in the area that no one was willing to buy except at a give-away price, and that would be just a drop in the bucket towards the ransom.

After receiving this last letter from the captors, Marina went to Villavo and succeeded in having an interview with Alvaro Garcia. She came back to San Martin, convinced that the situation was critical, and that we must make an immediate effort to get some money and make a larger offer. She contacted me in Bogota with the urgent request to get hold of five million pesos. The best that I could do was to get a promise from a wealthy businessman in Bogota, that he would loan us that amount on short notice should such an offer be accepted. I did not think that the kidnappers were going to budge from their persistent request of thirty million, and my hope for Russell's return was based on the military intervention. However on November 17 I sent a message to San Martin:

> Yes, Marina can offer 5 million, and I will get it as soon as necessary. However I do not believe that they will come down. They keep on asking such a high amount because they are convinced that we offered 20 million.

I felt very discouraged. Everything seemed hopeless.

Back in San Martin, Marina, Chaddy, Sharon, and Patty wrote a letter to the captors:

November 19, 1983

Señores:

Receive our greeting, extending it to Russell and hoping that this finds him well.

We want to inform you about the affair of the money. We have had many difficulties, but we have managed to get together four million pesos. We have persuaded some friends to loan us some funds. We beg you to have a little mercy with us for we have done all that is in our power to raise this sum.

Cordialmente,
La Sufriendo Familia
Stendal

On November 20, Chaddy took the letter to Villavo to be

sent to the captors, together with one that he wrote.

Señores Captores,

Receive my greeting. Remember that one day we all have to give an account to God for all that we have done. It is good to have this in mind at all times. Also have in mind that Jesus offers pardon to those who repent and ask for it. This doesn't mean to repent before the law, but before God.

In any case the decision is up to each one. This is very serious; it's the most important decision that exists in life. There is much to say to you, but I don't know if you want to hear it. Anyway, think seriously about all this. Thanks.

With love,
Chaddy

Besides waiting and praying for the guerrillas' response to these letters, I continued arrangements for the military rescue. I was convinced that this plan of action was our best hope. Once again I contacted the general. He gave me permission to come directly to his home inside the large military base and introduced me to his wife and family. It was clear that the general was now our personal friend, eager to do anything possible to secure Russell's release.

The lieutenant who had been assigned to lead the raid was on his leave to get married, but the general offered us the services of an officer he called "the best jungle fighter in the Colombian army," a veteran of four years guerrilla fighting in the jungle, involving countless battles. He arranged for us to meet this lieutenant, together with a major who was the airborne battalion's Intelligence officer. At the military airstrip we boarded the general's personal twin-engine airplane and prepared to make a pre-raid reconnaissance flight.

As the plane broke ground, I saw through my window something that caused me to immediately run up the aisle and shout in the pilot's ear, "Your left gas tank cover is off, and gasoline is pouring over the wing!" The pilot immediately circled and landed, and he secured the gas cap. It had been carelessly left off when the tank was refueled. 'Everyone involved in this operation was going to have to be a lot sharper than this, if we expected to get Russell out alive,' I thought. Safely airborne, we headed straight for Russell's location, and I moved up into the cockpit and navigated for the pilot. We headed straight for the transmitter in the backpack.

Jaime had connected the homing receiver to one of the airplane's antenna, and now he handed the receiver to the Intelligence officer. The major listened in utter fascination and amazement to the beep-beep.

We flew over Russell at 5,000 ft. There was no need to be lower, and we didn't want to arouse the guerrilla's suspicion of an impending raid. Along the river were small farm clearings, alternating with larger areas of solid jungle. The military officers were busy making sketches and plans. They selected a field several miles away from where Russell was held, where helicopters could land, but the sound would not be heard by Russell's guards. A small stream could be followed from the clearing to a spot within a few hundred yards of Russell's location. Chaddy would lead the men, using a hand-held homing device that would point them straight to Russell.

I asked the lieutenant if he thought the operation feasible. "We'll need about seventeen men," he responded. "That will give us enough fire power to handle anything the guerrillas can throw at us. More than that number would be hard to control in the jungle, especially at night."

I then asked him how he felt about it. His answer was the Spanish equivalent of, "It'll be a piece of cake."

CHAPTER 28

A Spy in Our Midst

Around the end of October, a new person had joined our household. Marina's mother had spent a week in Mapiripan and a girl named Cecilia had made friends with her. This girl had a sad story. She was from a family who lived in a very isolated area downriver from Chaparral. She claimed a problem had arisen, which made it necessary for her to leave her home area. A friend had arranged a job for Cecilia in Mapiripan. But since the "job" turned out to be in a house of prostitution, Cecilia rejected it, and now she said, she had no place to go, no job, and no money. She begged Marina's mother to take her to San Martin and help her find work.

Marina's mother felt that we could use additional help at this time, as Marina and Patty were so involved in the negotiation, and so she sent Cecilia to live with us. Gloria gladly shared her bedroom, but Marina cautioned us to say nothing about the kidnapping within Cecilia's earshot.

In previous years, we'd had other Colombian girls living with us and working for us from time to time, but we had never met anyone like Cecilia. In the first place she didn't look like a country girl; neither did she look like a city girl. She was short, stocky, strong, and athletic. She was poised, intelligent, and fairly well-educated for a country girl, but completely unsophisticated and unacquainted with many amenities of civilization. She had a short, nondescript hairdo, and her normal attire was well-fitting blue jeans and a T-shirt. Her customs were very strange.

168

The first thing we noticed was that she got up and started her work at four o'clock every morning. She made a lot of noise as she banged and rattled pans in the kitchen. When the rest of the family got up about 6:00 or 7:00, the house had been swept and mopped, and Cecilia was in the kitchen, ready to serve coffee, tea, or hot chocolate. However, at 6:30 P.M., as the night fell, Cecilia's eyes would droop, and she could hardly stagger over to Patty to ask permission to go to bed.

In her work in the kitchen, she was unbelievably clumsy with breakable objects. Most girls broke drinking glasses regularly, but this was a record: Cecilia broke four dozen glasses and two dozen cups in the two months she was with us. She insisted that she knew no English but listened carefully whenever we spoke that language in her presence. We soon discovered that she was eavesdropping when we talked to Chaparral on the radio.

We also noticed that Cecilia would hide in the kitchen whenever we had visitors from the Chaparral area. She did not want to go out on the streets of San Martin, and the few times it was absolutely necessary, she changed her accustomed blue jeans for an ill-fitting, shapeless housedress and arranged her hair as differently as possible. She evidently didn't want to be recognized.

Jaime was the first one to alert us. "You better get rid of that girl," he advised. "It looks to me like she has been planted here by the guerrillas to inform on you."

At first we were incredulous, but then other strange traits attracted our attention. Gloria reported that Cecilia slept well until about midnight. Then she spent time standing by the window. If she noticed Gloria was awake, she would go back to bed, but after a little while, she would be at the window again. "What are you looking out the window for?" Gloria asked.

"Oh, I don't have a watch, so I don't know what time it is, and I don't want the daylight to catch me in bed," Cecilia jokingly responded.

What was Cecilia doing? Was she picking up information and passing it on to someone who came to her window at night? Once Patty hid in the chicken yard well before dawn, waiting to see if someone came to the window, but she saw no one.

One day Cecilia sent a letter to Mapiripan with one of Marina's sisters. Was this a secret communication? The Espitias steamed it open, but its contents seemed harmless. We can't go on like this; we will have to send her away, we reluctantly decided. But Chaddy didn't agree. "All the better if she is a guerrilla spy," he insisted. "What better way of feeding information back to them? Let's keep her and use her as a line of communication to send the messages that we want them to have," Chaddy argued.

Patty decided to spend more time with Cecilia in the kitchen. Patty has a friendly personality and is usually able to bring people into her confidence fairly easily. "You know, I have another son besides Chaddy," Patty commented to Cecilia one day. "He is Marina's husband and Lisa's father, but he has been kidnapped and is being held by the guerrillas out in the jungle."

As if on cue, Cecilia turned around and cried with emotion, "Oh, *Señora* Patricia, pay them whatever they ask and get him out! He is suffering terribly!"

"But we can't pay it," Patty responded. We don't have that much money."

"Borrow it! Borrow it! Do anything to get it!" Cecilia continued. Patty sadly shook her head. She assured Cecilia that there was no way to meet the guerrillas' demands.

Chaddy and I went to Villavo to see how the Kirbys were getting along. During this period we never parked our vehicle in front of the place where we were going, as our old, red Toyota was well known. We slipped into the house where the Kirbys were, as inconspicuously as possible. Mrs. Kirby's release was still not generally known.

Rickey was overjoyed to see us and gave us each a big hug. She treated us more like intimate members of her family than just friends. She now knew after talking to Tom, the months of effort, risks, flights, and all that had been done in her behalf. Tom was also a very changed person. This old, weather-beaten rancher couldn't hold back the tears as he expressed his gratitude to us for bringing Rickey back to him.

Carefully I explained to him that by ourselves we were not naturally such helpful and compassionate people. Years ago we realized our deep spiritual need and confessed our failure to live the life God wanted us all to have. I continued to show how God had transformed our lives as we turned everything over to

Him. I could see by Tom's face that he was now, for the first time, understanding what real Christianity was. What God had done for me and multitudes of others, God could now do for him, I suggested. Indeed, God had already been working in Tom's life and had helped him make the difficult decision to use his very last cent to redeem his wife, Rickey, even though this would eventually leave both of them virtually penniless.

Chaddy then spoke up and told of his own experience and faith in God. He said, "Tom, there's a resistance we all have to the Gospel because of our pride. We must step over that line and turn everything over to Christ. It is very hard to do and takes a lot of courage, but it must be done." We prayed together for Tom, and I knew he needed time to absorb all the things that God was trying to teach him.

Meanwhile we were receiving distressing news from the Guaviare river area where the ranch was located. Many of our close friends were being killed. We decided to fly to the ranch to see if we could be of any help. We did not think the guerrillas would kill us, because then they would have no one to negotiate with and to raise money for Russell's release.

When I returned to San Martin, I sent out a letter to our friends in North America.

Lisa's first birthday party. Cecilia is the girl at extreme right.

CONFIDENTIAL
(Not to be released to the press or public
unless we are killed.)

Dear Friends,

The guerrillas are consolidating their control of the jungle area where Russell was kidnapped. They are not local people and are totally ruthless. They are members of the *Fuerzas Armadas Revolutionarios de Colombia* (FARC). This is the armed forces of the Communist Party. There are no army forces in the area.

Since this is a jungle area, inhabited only by Indians and homesteaders, there is no exploitation of workers or poor, hungry people. There are hundreds of miles of free, fertile jungle land here, so if anyone is hungry, it is because he does not want to work. All the reasons given in the predominantly leftist American press for guerrilla activity are missing here. What has happened is a Communist seizure of a vast area where the people do not want the guerrillas. They have seized the area by force and are killing and executing anyone who opposes them. They are obligating everyone in the area to pay taxes, amounting in many cases to an exorbitant percentage of the homesteader's income. If anyone has any resources, such as cattle, they kidnap the owner and demand an amount equal to the total value of his resources or more. Many of our friends have been killed. I will mention just a few.

Eduardo and Margarita had a little farm downstream from us. A Communist sympathizer had a quarrel with Eduardo about a few head of cattle and told the guerrillas about it. The guerrillas then came for Eduardo to kill him. I found out about it just before they were able to get to his place and dropped a note from the airplane telling him they were coming, but he decided to stay and defend his farm and property.

The guerrillas caught him and another man, tied them to a tree and shot them both in the stomach and in the head. They then contacted his wife, who happened to be about an hour away, and told her he had been executed by order of the people's court, and if she or her family gave any further resistance, they would all be killed. She requested the body but was refused.

Later the body was discovered in an isolated area, abandoned where he had been shot. Chaddy sent someone to attempt a proper burial. Eduardo had been one of Chaddy's friends for many years. When Margarita returned to the little farm, she found a note written by her husband before he was taken away. He wanted her to be sure the children grew up to be real Christians.

This couple had stayed at our house in San Martin a number of times. Margarita told me that Eduardo, who for many years had been rejecting the things of the Lord, had recently had a change of heart and was actually kneeling each night beside the bed of each child, praying with each one and reading the Bible.

I told Chaddy to get out of that area before they killed him, and he said, "Dad, someone has to stay and be a good testimony to these people at this difficult time." There was nothing more to say. All his life I have been telling him he must obey the Lord's voice and do what was right, regardless of the difficulties. He has stated that he doesn't want any ransom paid if he is captured.

In the nearest town people hear shots in the night. In the morning they find bloody places, and the bodies are gone, probably dumped in the river. About a third of the people have fled the area. Not one word has appeared in the Colombian papers about this violence, and nothing will, unless the people organize some resistance to the guerrillas. Then the newspapers will be filled with indignant denouncements of right-wing death squads and violations of human rights.

Soon after our return from the jungle, a sad story reached San Martin. About ten miles upstream from our ranch is the farm of a Christian family where Russell and I have preached and held meetings several times. The guerrillas arrived and asked to see the two older sons. They then took them out in the woods and shot them. The crime of these men was that they had complained in town to other homesteaders about the high taxes the guerrillas were charging them. The family brought the bodies to San Martin for burial. Patty and Marina attended the funeral. Few men attend funerals these days, as many times appearing at the funeral of an executed person causes you to be the next victim, since it may be assumed that you hold the same views that caused the dead man to be killed. The bodies were too decomposed to be brought into the church, so the funeral was held at the cemetery. The service was held as far away from the two coffins as possible. Patty and Marina's hearts ached for the parents and widows, one of whom was pregnant, and the other with three young children. When the family sadly returned to their farm after the funeral, they found that someone had stolen their dishes, blankets, and everything they had.

On November 29th, we heard from the kidnappers again. The news was good and bad. The good: their demand was lowered to twelve million, and the deadline was extended to December 25. The bad: it was their last demand. The note was written by a different hand, very hard to decipher, but the message was unmistakable. "If you do not meet our demand, we sadly inform you that we will not be responsible for the life of Russell." The death threat had been put into words.

I finished my letter to our friends back home:

> In regard to Russell's kidnapping, they have lowered their demands from $300,000 dollars to $125,000 dollars. Most of our friends in the States have felt that no ransom should be paid, so that the guerrillas will not be tempted to kidnap other Americans. The guerrillas don't reason that way. They will kidnap any American they can get hold of, and if they can't pay a ransom, they will be happy to kill them as hated representatives of what is to them a decadent capitalist society.
>
> Our not paying ransom may actually be causing deaths among the people, since the army is waiting until we get Russell out of the guerrillas' control before moving in. So we have decided to sell anything we can and use this along with any money specifically designated for ransom to try and negotiate his release. Hopefully they may come down a little. The guerrillas have kidnapped dozens of people in this area. They have all been released unharmed on payment of ransom. They have set a deadline of December 25 for this payment.
>
> It looks like this is going to be a difficult Christmas. We appreciate your continued prayers.
>
> Sincerely in Christ,
> Chad Stendal

When I returned from the jungle, I was saddened to hear that Tom Kirby had died. Patty and I went to Villavo to visit

Rickey. As we drove along the familiar road, Patty expressed what we were both thinking, "How sad that Rickey should lose her husband less than three weeks after her release." However, when we arrived at the missionaries' home where Rickey was still staying, we found that she was standing up under this ordeal amazingly well. She immediately told us of Tom's conversion.

"I told Tom he needed to turn his life over to the Lord, and he sincerely prayed with me as I held his hand, just before he died. The Lord led me to exactly the right moment to speak to him about his soul," Rickey told us.

Actually there were many factors leading to Tom's final conversion. Through the years a number of missionaries had cultivated a friendship with Tom and Rickey. The loving care given to Tom in his last months by the missionaries in Villavicencio must have played an important part. It was just like the Bible says: One plants, another waters, and God gives the increase.

Soon after Tom's death, Rickey decided to return to the States. All the things she loved so dearly in Colombia had been taken from her. The Kirby situation was resolved with finality, but now we were in the most desperate phase of our long and arduous negotiation for Russell's release.

Pat and Chad Stendal today.

CHAPTER 29

Who Is in Control?

Next to our faith in God, we took comfort from the letters of our friends. Especially consoling was the advice from our British friend, Mark Bles: "All their threats and horrors . . . must be taken with a pinch of salt, with bluff in mind. Do *not* believe *anything* they say on face value." A few days later his second letter arrived.

It was a tremendously encouraging letter. He counseled us to steel ourselves against the threats, including the deadlines. A graph was included, plotting the guerrillas demands against our offers, and he made the estimate of a settlement in early January at around $75,000 dollars. Of course we didn't have the $75,000 dollars, but just the fact that he could predict a final settlement at this amount, at this time when the captors were still holding to astronomical figures, gave us hope.

Mark advised us to make increases at a slow steady rate, tapering off as we got to our maximum. His last paragraph read:

Anyway you are all constantly in our thought, and we trust and pray everything is going as well as such horrors can do. Of all the families I have seen suffering through kidnap, yours is the best equipped; not the money, for you haven't that, but you have the strength of your faith to hold you steady when desperate hopes are shredded in pieces. Keep going, we're right behind you.

He also counseled us to feed information back to the guerrillas by any "grapevine" we could find. "Hearing by means of

177

other people that the Stendal family could not raise the ransom would carry more weight to convince the kidnappers than Chad's letters." Chaddy had been right about keeping Cecilia.

Cecilia gradually became more open with Patty as they worked together in the kitchen. She admitted that her male relatives were all in the guerrilla movement, and her father had been killed by them. Patty stifled the urge to ask her if she herself were a guerrilla, deciding it would not be wise to be so direct. Cecilia told Patty that the guerrillas had taken over the entire area where her family lived a number of years ago. "We got along quite well," she told Patty one day, "until the Russians came. Then everything became more difficult."

As Patty struggled to conceal her surprise, Cecilia went on to tell how the coming of three Russian advisors[1] had complicated the lives of her people. She implied that she had had a personal problem with one of the Russians and had fled for that reason. Was Cecilia actually in danger of being killed by the Communists? Or was she a member of the FARC who had been sent to spy on us? Perhaps both were true. Patty felt moved to offer refuge to Cecilia. "If you don't want to go back there again, we can take you to a place where you would be safe, and we could give you work there." Cecilia did not answer. Patty's plan was to send her up to the Sierra Nevada to work for Amanda.

Even though every moment seemed occupied with the negotiation and the planning of the military rescue, Patty decided to present a showing of our twelve "Life of Christ" movies, three a night. We hoped it would be a good way to communicate the Gospel to Cecilia, who had not had religious training in her background. The problem was to keep Cecilia from going to sleep. She still insisted on rising before 4:00 A.M. The first evening Patty had to stop the film several times and go find Cecilia, who had gone to bed. However, the second evening she showed more interest. After the last pictures of the crucifixion and resurrection, Sharon found her sobbing in the bedroom, "They killed God, and we are still suffering the consequences."

---

[1]It seems incredible that three Russians could visit a jungle area held by the guerrillas, however there were about 50,000 people of German and Polish descent in Colombia, and some of these had worked in the jungle. So three more foreigners would not draw undue attention in the jungle, as might be supposed.

Sharon told her that Jesus' death and resurrection has much meaning for us. She explained that since we have broken God's law, we deserve to die; however, Christ died for us so that He can forgive our sins, and so that the power of His resurrection could strengthen us to live a life pleasing to God. She explained that this is accomplished by turning away from wrong doing letting the same Christ, who lived a holy and just life almost 2,000 years ago, live that same life in us today.

As Cecilia listened she became more calm. Now she could see why we were so different from others she had known. She had received many new ideas these last few days. She would have much to think about.

In the early days of December, we received a telephone call from our good friend, Fred Stamey, in the United States. He and his wife, Marilyn, had worked tirelessly on our behalf, keeping people informed of our needs as the situation developed. Fred told us that two different donors had communicated their desire to contribute funds designated for ransom only. They wanted to know if we would accept the gifts on that basis, and if it turned out that we didn't pay ransom, would we return the money? Of course we agreed, and the process was started of transferring the funds to Colombia. The two gifts totaled $40,000, a little more than four million pesos, which was our current offer. How we praised the Lord for providing the money! Many other people were contributing as well, and it all began to add up. We sent a letter to Russell's captors offering 4 million 800 thousand pesos.

Meanwhile we continued to plan the details of the military raid. At a secret meeting in the Officers' Club, the logistics of making three helicopters available and other details were worked out. One helicopter would drop off the rescue team. Two others would stand by with reinforcements in case they got into a shooting encounter with a superior force and got pinned down. Police helicopters would be used, so that if anyone saw them flying or landing, they would assume it was a drug-field irradication operation, and not a rescue attempt. We knew the guerrillas had radio communication throughout the jungle.

The rescue team would be let down on the edge of the clearing that had been selected, and the men would immediately enter the jungle, as the helicopter returned to a safe area. From then on, travel would be only at night. Militarily speaking, I had one great reservation. As Chaddy would be leading the rescue team, homing in on Russell at night, I felt he needed two items of special equipment to be able to handle any contingency. One was a pistol with a silencer; the other was a night vision scope. The team hoped to silence Russell's closest guard by sneaking up on him at night and capturing or rendering him unconscious. We knew that if he or the rescue team fired a single shot, the whole guerrilla camp would mobilize for action. I felt they needed the capacity to shoot the guard, using a silenced pistol with a night scope, if they were in danger of being fired upon by the guard. The Colombian army had neither available.

As I began to pray about all these various details, the incongruity of a missionary praying for the Lord to help him obtain a silenced pistol became painfully clear. I was sent to Colombia by the Lord to evangelize an Indian tribe, not to shoot up guerrillas. I wondered if the whole idea of relying on a military solution was a spiritual trap. I thought to myself: how did I ever get into such a frame of mind as to even consider such a plan of action? I had been peacefully going about the Lord's work with Indians and colonists, preaching the Gospel and helping everyone I could. I began to wonder how I had ever gotten myself into a course of action where it could easily be necessary to shoot a number of people.

The Colombian military officers had been tremendously impressed with the homing and tracking device and wanted additional sets of this equipment for their own use. We put them in touch with Ralph, and in early December he arrived in Colombia bringing with him the additional equipment. He anticipated possible problems clearing customs, but when he announced that he was Colonel Ralph Burton of the U.S. Army bringing special equipment for General Roca, they ushered him right through.

Ralph was eager to help in any way he could. He was ready for any eventuality. He had with him his full camouflage field uniform and jungle boots. He had also brought a stainless steel 357 Magnum revolver. This last item caused me great shock.

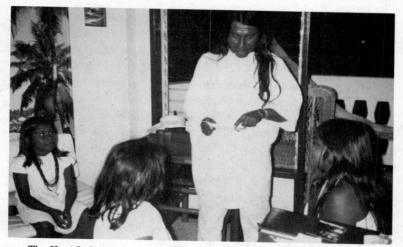

The Kogi Indians also prayed for Russell's release. Here a Kogi leader explains the Sermon on the Mount to other Kogis in Santa Marta.

"Ralph," I said, "if you had been caught carrying that weapon without a permit, as you passed through any of the military checkpoints to get here, they could have put you in jail for two years."

Ralph's presence put the military solution back on the front burner. Together we visited the military again. As he went over all the details of the rescue plan and became aware of the extremely difficult terrain, he began having doubts.

Ralph also visited the American Embassy. He found that they were very concerned about our situation, but there was nothing they could do. They now understood that any action on their part would only increase the risk to Russell's life.

As Ralph considered the negotiation option, he felt very strongly that something should be done to prevent the use of the money by the guerrillas. He had several ideas. Among the options he suggested was the use of counterfeit money. Ralph also knew about a chemical that could be used to treat the bills so that they would disintegrate the next day. We all chuckled, thinking of the guerrillas happily handling their money and seeing it disappear before their eyes. The only thing wrong with this option was that our whole family had better have disappeared out of Colombia at the same time.

Another idea Ralph had was to offer something poisonous to the guerrillas at the time of the ransom payment. Hopefully Russell would be out of their hands before they all dropped dead.

We moved ahead on both fronts at the same time, planning the military intervention and also continuing with the negotiation. We felt that as we "walked in the Spirit", God would direct us when the point of decision arrived. We decided that the most opportune time for the rescue operation would be the night of December 31. The guerrillas would be celebrating New Year's Eve, which is a big occasion in Colombia, and would likely be drunk and off guard.[2]

On December 9th we wrote to the *captores* again, raising our offer to 5 million 100 thousand pesos. Chaddy was not available to deliver the letter, so I took it to Alvaro Garcia in Villavicencio.

The meeting was set up in a grubby, third-rate restaurant. I asked for Garcia by name. Everyone seemed astonished and frightened. They were very upset that I had come instead of Chaddy, and I was told to go to another restaurant a block away. I later realized this detour permitted them to see if I were being followed.

Alvaro Garcia, looking very distraught and nervous, finally met with me. He was a plump man with a very disagreeable temperament. I didn't like his looks, and he didn't like mine. He tried to explain to me that he was just trying to help out in the negotiation. I explained to him our status as missionaries, and that we were not rich people. In fact, I told him that we were having considerable trouble raising money.

Garcia was obviously only involved in this negotiation for his own personal profit. From this time on, I began to suspect him of maneuvering to be in a position to intercept part of the ransom money for himself.

We did not hear from the kidnappers until December 19th, and when the letter arrived, it was dated December 5th, before our offer of December 9th.

---

[2]See Rescue the Captors, pp. 176–181, for New Year's Eve in the guerrilla camp.

Dec. 5, 83
Wilderness of Colombia

Señores y Señoras
Familiares de Martin

With the present (letter) we want to greet you and wish you success.

With this missive we want to inform you that we received your note. We tell you that the *Señor Martin* (Russell) is all right. But we also want you to know that we are not in agreement with your proposal. We continue insisting on the 12 million that we have proposed.

We will give you until the 25th of the present month as we have said before. And so we will expect to receive on the day of the 25th the delivery of the money agreed on. And if not, we will proceed to do that which we don't wish.

Attentively,
Captores

The letter was more delicately written, probably a feminine hand, but the message was sharp as a sword. We had had so much hope that they would accept our offer. The disappointment was cruel. We were reaching the upper limit of our possibilities.

The situation seemed desperate. It appeared that all the power was in the capricious hands of the guerrillas and we were impotent before them. Yet we knew that Christ had said, "All power is given to me in heaven and in earth."[3] We were not sleeping well. The entire situation hung over our hearts like a heavy, crushing weight. Brief lapses into the oblivion of sleep were a blessed relief, but waking brought the crushing burden again. One morning Patty jumped out of bed, as if to shake off the heavy load. "The guerrillas are not in control! God is in control!" she stated emphatically. This became her custom every morning from then on. THE GUERRILLAS HAVE TAKEN OUR SON! But they are not in control! GOD IS IN CONTROL![4]

---

[3]Matthew 28:18.
[4]In the guerrilla camp, the leader felt he was losing control of the situation. He accused Russell of trying to "take charge". *Rescue the Captors*, p. 177.

·CHAPTER 30

An Empty Place

After thinking about this last letter, I began to realize that there was no proof that it came from Russell's kidnappers.

It could have been written by anyone—Alvaro Garcia for example, or a member of his family. The handwriting in this letter was quite different. The *captores* had never bothered to state a location in their previous letters, and the heading, "Wilderness of Colombia," at the top would be a likely ploy for someone in Villavicencio, trying to give authenticity to a falsified letter from the guerrillas. Furthermore, the letter contained no detailed instructions for the delivery of the money to the guerrillas. It was unlikely that they would order the money simply handed over to Alvaro Garcia in Villavo on December 25, as the letter seemed to imply. In Mrs. Kirby's case and in other kidnappings in the area, the money was always exchanged directly for the kidnap victim.

It was entirely possible that the *captores* had reduced their demand, but the Garcia family had rewritten the letter before giving it to us, keeping the demand the same. I realized too that there was nothing to stop Garcia from rewriting the letters that we were sending to the guerrillas as well. If he could extract a larger sum from us than the guerrillas demanded, he could keep the difference for himself. It was too big a temptation for anyone of the caliber of Alvaro Garcia.

But what could we do? Our only contact with the guerrillas was now through this man. They had refused to negotiate in any other manner. I thought and prayed. How could I set up a system so that both the guerrillas and our family would know the true amounts at which each was negotiating? Suddenly I had an idea. I purchased a white T-shirt in Russell's size and a wide, blue marking pen.

It was now December 21. The deadline was on top of us. I made careful calculations and decided to make one last maximum offer to attempt Russell's release. My offer would be five million 500 thousand pesos—in dollars, $55,000[1] With the marking pen I wrote two large fives with a period between— 5.5—on the front of the white T-shirt. (This was a shortened form for 5.500.000[2], which the guerrillas would understand.) Then I wrote this letter to the guerrillas.

December 21, 1983

Señores Captores,

We hope that you are well, together with Russell. We received your last note which we find dated December 5, 1983. Because of the date, we believe that this is not an answer to our communication of December 9, 1983.

How sad and painful is our situation because of our great difficulty in getting money together, and to keep in our hands that which we offered you on December 9, (5.100.000).

Friends who have loaned us money do not believe that Russell is still alive and want their money back. Understand that I cannot sustain this offer for very long. Russell's grandmother, my mother, has become very sick, and I see that I must offer her attention and help. What can I do? In order for us to retain the money that we already have, we must have a new proof that Russell is alive. We are sending this T-shirt with the amount of our offer. You must write the number of your minimum demand under ours. Then take a photograph of Russell wearing the T-shirt with the numbers in front, clearly visible.

We also need a new letter from Russell. We hope that you will understand our situation and accept our offer of

---

[1] In dollars this would be the same as the Kirbys had paid. The peso/dollar exchange rate had increased since October.

[2] In Colombia, periods are used instead of comas to separate hundreds, thousands, and millions.

today, which is all that we are able to get together: 5 million 500 thousand pesos.

Cordially,
The Stendal Family

We had made our last offer. That was all we could do. Ralph, after full investigation and study of the military situation, informed us that in his opinion, there was only a fifty/fifty chance of Russell's surviving a military rescue, even if extremely well-executed. He felt our present situation was not promising, and he left Colombia to spend Christmas with his family.

Up until now, we had made no preparations for Christmas. After a family discussion, we decided that Russell would want us to have a Christmas dinner. Patty, Sharon, and Gloria decided to bake some Christmas goodies, and Chaddy and I located some chickens to roast. A few small presents were purchased, and the Christmas tree was set up. Cecilia was enlisted to go to town with Sharon and help carry back the purchases. Attired in her ill-fitting house dress, her arms full of groceries, she commented to Sharon, "You people certainly go to a lot of trouble for Christmas. Most people just buy a bottle of *aguardiente* (strong Colombian liquor)." But then she added thoughtfully, "I think your way is better."

Although few gifts were exchanged among us, we were all agreed that we wanted to give a present to Cecilia. "Get her a watch," suggested Gloria. "Then she will know what time it is, and we can see if she still gets up in the night to look out the window."

"That's a good idea," seconded Chaddy. "Get a good one, and then when she shows it to the guerrillas, they will know we don't exploit the people who work for us."

Christmas Eve we joined in prayer for Russell. We asked that his life be spared and for his safe return to us, but also for courage and grace for both him and us to endure whatever was necessary. Christmas Day, we roasted the chickens and moved the kitchen table into the dining room so that everyone could sit down to eat together. Gloria and Sharon insisted that Cecilia join us, but she held back until Chaddy and Pat added their urgings too. Then flushed and smiling, she sat down with us, her new watch around her wrist. We set an empty place at the table for Russell. He was very much in our thoughts and prayers.

Christmas Day ended, and there was no communication from the guerrillas. Chaddy and I took off in the plane to fly over the guerrilla headquarters and listen to the beeper again. As we flew over the now familiar terrain, I meditated on our problem. We did not have even half enough money to meet the guerrillas' demand. The military rescue seemed the only way out. As we neared the spot, I saw that there was a peculiar cloud formation right over the guerrilla headquarters. We could only pass over once in a straight line, so as to appear to be just any airplane in flight going across the area, but because of the clouds, I was forced to go down under them to an altitude of about 250 feet.

As I was listening to the familiar beep, Chaddy yelled, "You're going too low! They'll recognize us!"

It was too late; I didn't know the cloud would force us so low. (But, somehow, in my spirit I felt sure that I was doing the right thing.) Dangerously visible, Chaddy and I both realized that Russell would recognize the sound of the Cessna 170 and would probably see it from the ground. Its rounded tail was different from all other planes. We were hoping that he would be strengthened to endure whatever difficulties he was experiencing. He would also be alerted to the possibility of a military raid and hopefully would be ready to leave at an instant's notice and to help in any way he could.

We later learned that Russell and the guerrillas did see our plane. When the guerrilla leader questioned Russell, he answered, "Whether that was my father's airplane or not, I can tell you one thing. You had better settle this negotiation rapidly and accept whatever he is offering. I know my father, and I know what he can do. You're going to be in for a raid."

The guerrillas were now very concerned that their main headquarters had been discovered and military helicopters would soon descend for a rescue in force.

On New Year's Eve, Chaddy was called to Villavo to receive another communication from the kidnappers. He returned with a letter from the *captores*, dated December 28, the day after our flight over the camouflaged guerrilla center. It stated that they were accepting our offer. They indicated that Russell was sick, and they wanted to get him off their hands as quickly as possible.

They had not been able to photograph Russell in the T-shirt, they said, because it had not been sent to them, but as proof that he was still alive, they were sending a letter in Russell's handwriting. The details of the exchange were disturbing. They wanted Chaddy to fly the plane into guerrilla territory, bringing the money.

Now we had crucial decisions to make. In the first place, Chaddy wasn't a pilot. He returned to Villavo to consult with Alvaro Garcia, and he obtained guerrilla permission for me to fly the plane. Alvaro Garcia was to come to San Martin to meet us at 8:00 A.M. January 2. He would give us our destination where we were to meet the guerrillas, only when we were in the air.

We were disappointed that we didn't receive the photo we had requested. The letter was really not an adequate proof that Russell was still alive. It contained nothing of importance, and could have been written anytime previously. We studied the letter, prayed and analyzed the situation. Had they forced Russell to copy the letter, and then killed him on Christmas Day as they had threatened? If this were the case, they would now be able to take Chaddy and the money. Why had they not sent us the photograph of Russell in the T-shirt? Did this prove the treachery of Alvaro Garcia, that he didn't dare send them the shirt, or had they received the shirt but not photographed Russell because they had killed him? Should we accept this offer, or would it be better to refuse it and carry out the military raid?

As I considered the two options, I wasn't happy with either one. Why had it been possible to find out Russell's location, if we were not to use this information to rescue him? I was totally confused. I began to pray all the more earnestly for the Lord's solution to this dilemma. Chaddy also was confused. It was clear that the Lord would have to show me as head of the family what should be done.

We studied the letter from Russell again, looking for clues. The letter was in cursive writing, definitely Russell's, but the date was in manuscript letters. I was afraid the letter had been written previously and the date added later by another person. Patty studied the date carefully, "I think this is Russell's writing," she mused. All of a sudden she shouted, "I know it was Russell that wrote this date! Look here! December is abbreviated 'Dec.'. Only an English speaker would do that. If a guerrilla had written in the date later, they would have written 'Dic.', the Spanish abbreviation for *Diciembre*. Russell wrote the date, and without thinking, wrote the abbreviation in English instead of Spanish."

So on the evidence of the one English vowel, we decided that the letter was an authentic proof that Russell was still alive.

After a crucial time of very serious prayer on this life-or-death matter, the Lord made things more clear to me. We needed to rely on Him to release Russell, if that was His will, and not rely on all kinds of intricate military plans. If the Lord had called Russell as a missionary to the guerrillas, then we certainly had no business doing a military solution. It would actually be better for all of us to lay down our lives for the Gospel, than to take precipitous action that God had not directed. I talked over this decision with the family. All were in agreement, and Chaddy said he was willing to take the ransom money and meet with the guerrillas.

New Year's Day was spent in getting ready for the delivery of the ransom. At this time of the year, all commerce closes down for days, and banks are closed. Fortunately, I had the five million 500 thousand pesos ready, hidden in a wall safe that I had installed behind a large picture of Spirit Island in the Canadian Rockies in our bedroom.

Not one of our friends who was interested in tricking the guerrillas was available for consultation. Ralph was home in Minnesota. Jaime was out of reach in Bogota.

I sent Patty and Sharon to Villavo to advise the general of the recent developments. His teenaged sons informed them that their father was at the hospital, at the bedside of his young daughter who had just had an emergency appendectomy. He could not be disturbed. We were on our own. We had no chemicals to make the money disappear, no poison, no knock-out drops, no counterfeit bills. We had to play it straight, and this is what I really felt we should do anyhow.

Patty was distressed about the risk that Chaddy was taking. She sat down with her Bible, asking God for wisdom and assurance that we were doing the right thing. As she paged through the Bible, reading here and there, a marked verse caught her eye. She had marked it in her Bible just before we left for Colombia in 1964, feeling that God had indicated that it had special significance for us. It was Isaiah 49:25:

> *Even the captives of the mighty shall be taken away,*
> *And the prey of the terrible be delivered;*
> *For I will contend with him who contends with you,*
> *AND I WILL SAVE YOUR SONS.*

This verse gave her strength and confidence for the ordeal of the next two days.

Patty, however, was still obsessed with the idea of sending something to the guerrillas. She was still thinking of poison or knock-out drops, so that Chaddy and Russell could grab the money and flee after all the guerrillas were overcome. She went into the bedroom to pray about what we could do to the guerrillas.

Meanwhile Gloria was in the kitchen baking chocolate chip cookies. She thought that Russell would enjoy something typically American when he arrived home after his long captivity. About 2:00 A.M., as Patty was still praying, she felt God wanted us to send the guerrillas the chocolate chip cookies.

The next morning Marina and Patty packed some of the cookies in a holiday canister, decorated with a big blue bow and a New Year's card. Marina wrote a message on the card, thanking the guerrillas for their good treatment of Russell. "We don't know if they treated him well or not, but we'll give them the benefit of the doubt," Marina remarked after inscribing the card. They also packed a box of leftovers for Russell from our New Year's Day dinner—cold chicken and dressing—and of course, the cookies. Both packages were made up of delicious ingredients—no knock-out drops.

CHAPTER 31

The Guerrillas Have Both Sons

January 2, 1984

We waited impatiently for Alvaro Garcia to show up. He was to arrive at 8:00 A.M., but he didn't come. Earlier that morning we had checked over the old Cessna 170 very carefully. There could be no slip up. Russell's life and many things more lay in the balance.

The police guarding the San Martin airstrip eyed us carefully. We wanted them to believe that this was a routine flight. If they suspected anything or searched us and found the ransom money, we would probably never see that money again. At the very least, it would be impounded, and the guerrillas would kill Russell for our not delivering the ransom. Hour after hour went by, and we were getting very worried. I drove our jeep around town to look for Garcia. Finally at 11:00, he arrived at the appointed destination.

"Where in the world have you been?" I asked.

He looked a little worried and said, "This is the day after New Year's, and most people, including taxi and bus drivers, haven't sobered up yet, so I couldn't get transportation."

We immediately drove by the house and picked up the duffel bag full of money. It was quite heavy. Chaddy swung it over his shoulder as he nonchalantly walked from the jeep to the plane under the watchful eyes of the police.

Finally, we were all in the plane, and, as I started the engine, the negotiator gave us our destination. It was an isolated

191

airstrip within guerrilla-held territory. I had never landed there. "I hope I can find it," I replied.

I began to be apprehensive. The guerrillas were expecting us at 10:00 A.M., and it would be almost 1:00 P.M. before we would arrive. Would they still be waiting?

When we approached the rendezvous, it was hard to see the airstrip, which was secluded in a very remote area. I landed the plane, and immediately we were approached by a jeep with a number of children passengers[1], as well as a sly-looking driver, wearing mirror surface sun glasses. Chaddy and Garcia got out of the plane to talk to them, and soon Chaddy returned for the duffel bag and said, "They say to come back tomorrow at 9:00 A.M., and you should be able to pick up me and Russell." Chaddy turned and left with the people in the jeep. If he was worried, he certainly didn't show it. I took off for home with my heart in my throat. Now the guerrillas had both my sons.

To get back to San Martin, I had to fly directly over Lomalinda, the Wycliffe Bible Translation Center. My good friend, Jim Walton, was now director, and I decided to drop in and advise my friends of the present developments. Jim and his family were also from Minnesota, and we had gone through the Wycliffe Jungle Camp in Mexico together. Just twenty years before, we had all arrived in Colombia. "Jim," I said, "now the guerrillas have Russell and Chaddy and the money, and tomorrow they have an opportunity to trap me and the plane as well."

"Well," Jim said, "We'll pray all night. When you return from the guerrillas tomorrow, wiggle your wings as you fly over, if you have Russell. If he is sick, (as he was reported to be) you may not want to stop, but we will be anxiously awaiting the outcome."

Finally I arrived at San Martin. An impossibly long night awaited us. Neither Patty nor I could sleep. Sharon, Gloria, Marina, and everyone in the house awaited the outcome with painfully intense anticipation.

The next morning rose dark and grey with some rain. What if I were weathered in? The flight would take just one hour. I

---

[1]The guerrillas had the children in the car to ensure that the army would not fire upon them in case they had somehow followed our plane.

took off just at 8:00 A.M. I did not wish to be either early or late. On the horizon was one little patch of lightness about ten degrees wide in a sea of grey. I swung the plane onto its heading, and I was lined up with the light on the horizon. The closer I got to the destination, the lighter it got. Just before I flew over the guerrillas' strip, I flew out from under the clouds into intensely blue sky with the sun shining down with unusual brightness.

I strained my eyes to see if my two sons were on the strip. There below me was Chaddy, waving his hat, which was our signal that everything was all right. Standing next to him, low and behold, was Russell, waving everything he had! I put the plane into an abrupt slipping spiral and came down like an elevator. "Thank you, Lord! Thank you!" I shouted. It was the most emotional moment of my life, as I opened the door to receive my sons who were running toward the plane.

Then I noticed two men running less than 100 yards behind them. "Who are they?" I asked Chaddy.

"I don't know! We'd better get out of here!" he replied. I spun the plane around with the boys aboard and covered the two men with dust. The gutless wonder seemed to catch our enthusiasm and sprung into the air like a jackrabbit.

As we approached Lomalinda, I knew all the people there were anxiously awaiting the news, so I asked Russell, "Would you like us to land at Lomalinda? The people there have been praying for you all night."

He agreed, so I landed and taxied up to the hangar and found many of our old friends straining to see if we had Russell aboard. What a tremendous welcome he received. Everybody was hugging him, and some had tears of joy. Finally we all joined hands and sang the hymn of praise, "How Great Thou Art." It was January 3, exactly twenty years ago to the day that Jim Walton and I, together with our families, had arrived in Colombia for the first time. What an anniversary!

We didn't linger long there, however, because we knew the rest of the family were all still anxiously awaiting us in San Martin.

"Come on, Russ, we've just got to go," I said as he tried to pry himself away from the eager grasps of many friends.

"I want to fly the plane back to San Martin," he replied. "I have dreamed for months of flying a plane again."

I wasn't sure of his physical condition after such a long captivity, but he was so insistent that I went to the right side of the plane, and he slipped into the pilot's seat. A look of exuberance and pure joy was all over his face as he checked over the controls and started the engine. He taxied away as all our friends waved good-bye. Everyone was just so terribly happy for us. Russ soon had the old plane in the air, going through her paces as he tried the controls first this way, then that way, and then wheeled the plane around and pointed the nose down, aimed at the Lomalinda airstrip. I got a little nervous as the speed indicator approached the red line and we were in a power dive. I wasn't sure that Russell had recovered from the trauma of his captivity, and so when the wings started trembling from the high speed, I said, "Russell, are you all right?"

"I'm fine!" he replied while his hands forced the controls forward.

Finally the strip was coming right up, and I yelled, "Russell! If you don't pull up, we're going to be ten feet under the runway!"

"Don't worry! I've got everything under control!"

Actually he was handling things with the master touch of a veteran jungle bush pilot, and just before we would have crashed, he leveled the plane out, right on the deck, and sped just above the ground like a rocket, right in front of all our friends at Lomalinda. I guess he just wanted to put on an airshow for everybody, and then in an expression of pure exuberance and joy, he pulled the plane up in a sharp climb. Because of our extra speed, we went up, and up, and up, and finally, just before we stalled, he put the rudder in, and we gently fell off on a wing toward San Martin where his mother, sisters, wife, and daughter were waiting.

RUSSELL WAS FREE!

CHAPTER 32

Two Eldest Sons

As San Martin came into view, Russell prepared to land the old faithful 170. He was as happy to be flying again as if this were his first solo. It seemed like old times as he cut the engine, put down the flaps, and lined up with the runway—almost as if the previous four-and-a-half months had never occurred. I felt as if I were just awakening after a terrifying nightmare, only to find everything normal.

Russell made a perfect landing. And there, standing by the strip, was his trusted mechanic, Fidel. With remarkable reserve, Fidel said, "Glad to see you back, *Capitan*".

"You don't know how glad I am to *be* back!" Russell replied.

"Fidel risked his life to repair the 170 in Canyo Jabon, so we could fly it out," Chaddy added.

Our house was just a few blocks away from the airstrip. Marina and Patty were looking anxiously out the window and saw the plane land. Gloria and Sharon were on top of Chaddy's truck to get a better view. They still did not know if we had Russell or not. "Three people got out of the plane!" Gloria shouted, "One of them must be Russell!" Watching from the window, Marina and Patty also saw the three figures alight from the airplane.

"*Martincito! Martincito!*" screamed Marina, throwing her arms around Patty's neck.

On the way home from the strip, Russell asked how everyone was. "Everyone is fine, but don't be disappointed if Lisa doesn't recognize you. You've been away a long time, and she's only fourteen months old," I reminded him.

As Russell walked through the door, Lisa took one look at him and then came running. "¡*Papá*! ¡*Papá*!" she shouted. The resulting scene was too emotional to be described. After embracing his daughter and Marina, Russell took a good look at his mother's face. The tremendous joy of the occasion could still not hide the tired, worn-out look. Only the Lord knew how many hours she had spent in prayer.

But now the family was all back together again, stronger and more united than ever. How we praised the Lord for His watching over Russell, and indeed every detail of the long ordeal, resulting in his release. There was a lot of catching up to do. Russell related a few of his experiences, and it became clear that our prayers that he would be a good missionary to the guerrillas had been answered.

Later on, I was in our bedroom, and I overheard Russell talking to Chaddy in the next room. "Nobody ever had a better brother than you, Chaddy," Russell said, his voice trembling with emotion, "—risking your life for me."

I never knew how much I loved you 'til the guerrillas took you away," Chaddy responded. They both unashamedly hugged each other, with tears of emotion.

To me this was a greater miracle than all the rest. God had brought my two sons together, and I was profoundly moved, as I praised Him for it. After all, not many fathers have two eldest sons.

And the rains descended, the floods came and the winds blew and beat on that house (household) and it did not fall, for it was founded on the rock.[1]

It wasn't until after we had gotten Russell out of captivity that I could understand the biggest and most confusing aspect of the entire kidnapping. Why had we been able to find out Russell's exact location in the jungle, if we were not to do a military rescue?

I had spent many hours trying to resolve this problem; however, after talking with Russell, the situation became clear. He said that the guerrillas had panicked when our airplane flew very low over their location. This was their most secure stronghold and the headquarters for training recruits. Here above the series of waterfalls, they felt on home ground. The guerrillas

---

[1] Matthew 7:25.

always attacked the army from ambush, and when things got tough, they could always withdraw to this area and be safe. The last thing they wanted was an attack on their most important and secure location.

I believe the Lord caused the cloud to form over their head-quarters, so that I would fly low enough for them to see me and suspect that their position had been located. When I began flying under the cloud, I felt an assurance from the Lord that I was doing the right thing, even though I had not originally intended to fly nearly so close to them. The cloud forced me down low, right over the spot where they were holding Russell.

As you may recall, the guerrillas wrote a letter the very next day, accepting our offer at considerably less than half of what they had been asking and wanted us to receive Russell immediately. The U.S. invasion of Grenada had just taken place, and perhaps their informers had made them aware of Ralph Burton's visit as a high-ranking U.S. military officer. Well-armed as they were, they did not want to risk an attack on their stronghold, perhaps involving the U.S. military, as well as the Colombian army.[2]

After talking with Russell and learning how agitated the guerrillas became when the plane flew over, I was able to realize what had happened: The Lord enabled us to get the backpack into the guerrilla's stronghold and sent the cloud in just the right shape in order to secure Russell's release. Russell's location was not given to us for the purpose of conducting a military raid at all. It was given to encourage both Russell and our family at a time of great stress, and finally to panic the guerrillas into releasing Russell.

Now it was clear why we needed to be careful to listen to the Lord. If we had gone ahead with a military solution, as circumstances seemed to indicate, all the blessings and wide-open-doors for ministry that we have since experienced would never have occurred. Also, after talking with Russell, I realized that there were many more guerrillas in the area than we thought. Russell and Chaddy and all the commandos would probably have been wiped out, had the military operation been attempted with just seventeen men.

---

[2]See *Rescue the Captors* pp. 161–162.

Chaddy and Russell get on with their lives.

Epilogue

As Russell walked through the door, Cecilia saw him, and Gloria heard her mutter, "They were ordered to kill him, what happened?" When Patty entered the kitchen a few minutes later to check on lunch, Cecilia turned to her with great emotion and remarked, "You certainly have a lot of faith, *Señora Patricia*, to have received your son back again, alive."

A few hours later she came to Patty and stated, "I have to leave for Mapiripan. Will you take me to the station to catch the 5:00 A.M. bus?"

Patty expressed surprise at her leaving so suddenly. "Oh, I received a message from my mother that the person that was causing me the problem at home in the jungle has left. My mother is sick, and so I have to go," Cecilia explained. But we knew that no one had come with a message; there had been no communication from the jungle. We could only assume that with Russell's return, Cecilia's mission was finished.

As Patty put her on the bus the next morning, Cecilia told her sadly, "I would like to stay with you, *Señora Patricia,* but I can't. I have to go back to the jungle."

We assumed that she feared retaliation against her family if she didn't return.

The following morning Russell commented, "You can't believe all the noise the guerrillas make in the morning. They all get up at 4:00 A.M. and start banging things around. It never occurred to them to be quiet. If the army wanted to find them, all they would have to do is go out in the jungle with 'noise detectors' about four or five in the morning."

We told him that if Cecilia had not left that morning, he would have thought he was back in the guerrilla camp.

The next day Ricardo Trillos from the Reconciliation ministry came and took Russell and his family to Bogota. We felt left in an emotional vacuum after the high tension under which we had been living for so many weeks. Russell was planning to have a complete medical check-up. He was suffering from headaches, intensified by the rope which had been around his neck and shoulders all during his captivity.

However, the day before he was to enter the hospital in Bogota, we had to call him back to San Martin. Neftali Espitia, Marina's father, was taken ill. His health had been failing for several years, and it seemed that the strain and anguish of the kidnapping, the sleepless anxiety-filled nights, and the constant planning of ways to secure his son-in-law's release had taken their toll. Ten days after the joy of Russell's release, Marina and her family were plunged into the grief of Neftali's death.

Russell and Marina's sorrow was tempered by the knowledge that during the time of Russell's captivity, Neftali had committed his life and family to the Lord. Neftali's mother, Carmen, expressed faith in God for the first time in her ninety-plus years. When Russell went to visit her after his release, she told him with a rare smile, "I can see that you have forgiven your captors. You are not bitter about your experience. And so I am going to forgive those who have wronged me."

We were impressed with the similarity in the deaths of Tom Kirby and Neftali Espitia, each occurring some two weeks after the ordeals were ended. A kidnapping extracts a terrible emotional outlay from the suffering family. In one sense it is worse than a sudden death which one can come to terms with, and recover from, after the initial shock. The most cruel aspect of a kidnapping is the uncertainty of the fate of the loved one, especially when it extends over weeks, and months. A human being is not built for sustained emotional uncertainty of a deep, long-term nature.

Russell never did have his medical check-up, however. By the time he and Marina had helped the Espitia family cope with Neftali's sudden death, Russell was feeling fine and did not feel the need for a medical examination.

The next Sunday, Patty, Gloria and Uriel visited their friends in the under-privileged neighborhood. They told them the good news of Russell's release, and Patty read again the Bible verses that she had shared with them the first Sunday after Russell was captured. They could now all see how they had been fulfilled.

The people all rejoiced with her. They had been praying for Russell for almost five months, and in their simple faith each family was convinced that it had been their prayers that secured Russell's freedom. Their faith was greatly strengthened to bring their own desperate needs to God in prayer.

Chad accompanied Russell to the American Embassy in Bogota. The woman in charge of expediting the paperwork for the family's entrance to the United States turned out to be the same one who had visited us in San Martin. She too was delighted at Russell's safe return. She and Chad were reconciled and the unfortunate incident in Villavicencio was forgiven and forgotten.

Rickey Kirby is now living in Australia where she is effectively serving the Lord in her local church. However, her heart aches for Colombia and hungers for news of her dear neighbors and friends. Our daughter, Sharon, married Bob Jackson, an excellent linguist, and they with their two small sons continue to work with the Kogi Indians. Gloria married Uriel, and they are presently in the United States, training and working, awaiting the Lord's leading to return to Colombia.

Final Notes:

After the kidnapping, the guerrillas immediately suffered two of the worst defeats they ever experienced.

The main jungle center for refining coca paste into cocaine was captured and destroyed by the police just three weeks after Russell's release. This center processed most of the coca paste, not only from Colombia, but also from Bolivia and Peru as well. Over half of all cocaine used in north America and Europe came from there. This amounted to fifteen tons of cocaine a month. In an isolated area of Colombia, 200 miles in all directions from the nearest villages, the Medellin Cartel[1] operated a little, self-contained village with a 5,000 foot airstrip, boasting night lights and an instrument landing system.

---

[1] Wealthy Colombians who control the drug trade from the city of Medellin in northwestern Colombia.

The police arrived in helicopters with their specially-trained swat teams and defeated the guerrilla bands that were guarding the installation. They achieved complete surprise and seized 14.8 tons of cocaine, making this raid the largest drug bust in the world.

For the first time, the connection between the mafia and the guerrillas was irrefutably established, resulting in the new term, "narco-terrorism". The guerrillas actually were receiving part of the profits and were providing armed protection against the military and police in return.

The police seized all the records of those involved in this operation, establishing the identities of Medellin "businessmen" such as: Carlos Lehder, Ochoa, Escobar, and a host of others who were investing money in the lucrative drug trade. The losses suffered by the mafia and guerrillas was incalculable, but certainly involved billions of dollars.

The guerrillas, having suffered a loss of credibility in their military prowess, tried to rectify things with a spectacular, large-scale raid on the city of Florencia, the capital of the territory of Caqueta. They suffered the worst military disaster in their history, losing dozens of their best men. The only thing that saved them from a complete set-back in all of Colombia was the brilliant effort of their political arm, which negotiated a cease-fire with the government and secured amnesty. Unbelievably, this allowed more than four hundred captured guerrillas to leave prison, promising to return to civil life. They deceived the government advisers, and most of them soon returned to their guerrilla units.

The guerrillas were able to regroup their forces during the cease fire and have increased their military and political power to this day. They now control roughly eighty percent of the rural land area of Colombia.

They rule these areas with an iron hand, executing drug addicts, alcoholics, and all common criminals, as well as anyone who opposes them. They levy taxes, issue identity cards, and control all activity within these areas. These are totalitarian Communist countries within the democratic country of Colombia.

From the perspective of four years, looking back at the kidnapping, we can now see a large number of benefits that have accrued.

Russell's book, *Rescue the Captors* has now topped 40,000

copies sold. Over 13,000 copies in Spanish have been distributed in Colombia. We have received over 500 unsolicited letters stating how people were blessed by the book.

Chaddy took the Spanish version directly to the guerrilla leadership, offering to revise anything to which they objected as not factual. Amazingly they approved the book for distribution in the areas they control, and over 300 copies were distributed directly to the guerrillas. Through these guerrilla contacts, we secured religious liberty to evangelize in these areas, and this included liberty for other missions as well.

The ministry of all our family and our Colombian co-laborers has been multiplied many-fold. We are now respected and well-received throughout the sections of the *llanos* and jungle where we are working. Because we did not leave Colombia and head for home after the kidnapping, most people now understand that we are there because we love them and because we want them to be reconciled to God.

Chaddy continues to live at Chaparral in an area which is still controlled by the Communists. He has had a great influence for good on many of the guerrillas. Many are convinced of the existence of God, and some have come to have a personal faith in Jesus Christ. As Russell once said, "The guerrillas are like a tribe, and Chaddy has learned their language and culture." It is hard for them to be anti-North American when Chaddy is the most helpful person in the area. Chaddy is now married and has a baby daughter.

In May, 1986, Patty and Russell invited by the now legal political party called the Patriotic Union attended a Communist political rally in the jungle with Chaddy. Russell conversed with the leaders who questioned him about the Wycliffe Bible Translators Center at Lomalinda, which lay directly in the path of the Communist advance. Russell assured them that these American missionaries were not exploiting the Indians in any way, but only bringing them medical and educational aid, and the message of the Bible in their own languages. The Translation Center at Lomalinda is still in operation.

Patty presented four films from the "Life of Christ" series. Only one man was upset. Chaddy found him out on the edge of the clearing, trying not to look at the movie and muttering to himself, "By God, I'm an atheist!" As Chaddy pointed out to him the inconsistency of his statement, the leaders gathered to hear what was going on. Russell walked over in time to see Chaddy put his arm around the Communist leader from Villavicencio and say, "We believe in Jesus Christ, don't we?"

"Sure, Chaddy, sure," he responded.

Everyone happily went back to watching the picture, confident that it was all under the approval of the Communist party.

The reconciliation ministry—which started as family reconciliation with a first step of being reconciled to God through the Lord Jesus Christ—now has been greatly expanded to include National Reconciliation. That means we are working to reconcile guerrillas with the army and police, Liberals with Conservatives, and so forth.

The tremendous violence that Colombia is experiencing is causing many people to seek and cry out to God to deliver them and their country. We have now exceeded 100,000 in total attendance at the crusades and around 50,000 in special meetings in schools, armed forces bases, at women's seminars and the like. Russell and I have also had a greatly expanded ministry in the U.S. and Canada.

Looking back on the kidnapping, we can now say, *"They meant it for evil, but God meant it for good!"*

Appendix A

The Beatitudes[1]

Blessed are those who recognize their spiritual need because only[2] they will participate in the Kingdom of God.

Blessed are those who sorrow over their sins and the sins of others, because only they will be comforted.

Blessed are those who do not react with violence or rebel against God, because only they will inherit the earth.

Blessed are those who hunger and thirst after righteousness for only they shall be filled.

Blessed are those who show forgiveness and mercy, because only they shall receive forgiveness and mercy.

Blessed are the clean and pure in heart, for only they shall see and know God.

Blessed are those who work for reconciliation and peace for only they shall be called by God his sons (and daughters).

Blessed are those who willingly suffer persecution for the cause of righteousness, because only they will participate in the Kingdom of God.

Blessed are you when men insult you and persecute you, speaking all manner of evil against you falsely; Rejoice and be glad because great is your reward in heaven; in the same manner the prophets before you were persecuted as well.

---

[1] New, dynamic translation by Chad Stendal.
[2] In the Greek, the construction is emphatic giving this meaning.

Appendix B

The Test

On August 21, one week after Russell's disappearance, I wrote a letter to our friends in North America. I had just returned to San Martin from Canyo Jabon after our repair and recovery of the Cessna 170.

> "Though I walk through the valley of the shadow of death, I shall fear no evil, for thou art with me."
>
> How may times have we read this phrase without appreciating its full potential. I feel I understand the comfort of its promise much better today than ever before. . . .
>
> We do not fear the guerrillas who can only take our lives. *They* are in danger of losing their souls. We are praying for them, and we invite all our friends to do likewise.
>
> *"Love your enemies, bless them that curse you, do good to them that hate you, and pray for them which despitefully use you and persecute you."*

I felt definitely led of the Lord to include that verse. I asked Patty to locate the reference. "It's Matthew 5:24," she called back in a few minutes.

Then it hit me! This verse was from the Sermon on the Mount—the last part of the same chapter which started with the Beatitudes. Russell had been given insight and understanding on this portion of Scripture, but it wasn't enough to understand and preach it. He had to be put to the test. He had to live the Sermon on the Mount in order to have real authority and power to preach it.

Russell was not only called to be a witness to the guerrillas, he was being given an additional course in his training for living in the Kingdom of God—a chance to learn to love his enemies, bless them that curse him, do good to them that hate him, and pray for them that treat him badly and persecute him.

I felt a sense of awe in the presence of our All-Wise God, who was refining and polishing His servant, qualifying his character to preach on the Sermon on the Mount with authority and power, having experienced the trial of his faith. I prayed at that time that he would pass the test, that he would be able to love these guerrillas, no matter what they might be doing to him.

A Word from the Authors

This book has been difficult to write as it was necessary to go back and re-experience emotionally the traumatic time of Russell's captivity. Perhaps that is why it took us so long to write it. On the other hand, as we looked back into our notes and letters which we had saved from the time of the kidnapping, we were once again thrilled to see how truly God had everything under control.

We wish to thank the many, many people all over the world who upheld us during those difficult months. We have appreciated the help of Chaddy and Marina, who supplied us with their first-person accounts. Thanks too to Gloria for sharing her memories of that time and for her many hours of work on the manuscript. A special thanks to Arlin Becker who proofread the manuscript.

Most of all we give thanks to God who was with us in this ordeal and who causes "all things to work together for good." Our desire is that as you read this true story, you may be strengthened to withstand whatever trial may lay ahead in your life. The same God will be with you who was with us. Truly *He* is the hero of this story.

If you would like to have Chad and Pat, Russell and Marina, or Bob and Sharon speak at your church when they are home, please advise the Pan-America Mission. Chad, as a Bible Translator, is also giving seminars on Colossians, Titus, 1 John, or James to interested churches.

Those who would like to participate in this ongoing ministry and receive our periodic newsletter, may write to us at the Pan-America Mission, Inc., P.O. Box 16157, Portland, OR 97216.

Chad and Pat Stendal

Additional copies of this book may be obtained for $7.95 postpaid from Ransom Press, P.O. Box 1456, Burnsville, MN 55337.

Orders of 10 copies or more will receive a special discounted price of $6.95 per copy postpaid.